Writing Is Magic, Or Is It?

Using the Mentor Text to Develop the Writer's Craft

Authors

Jennifer M. Bogard and Mary C. McMackin

Foreword

Melissa Cheesman Smith

SHELL EDUCATION

Image Credits
istock: pp. 1, 3, 5, 6, 19, 47, 87, 107, 119,121, 134, and front and back cover ; All other images Shutterstock

___

Shell Education
5301 Oceanus Drive
Huntington Beach, CA 92649-1030
http://www.shelleducation.com
ISBN 978-1-4258-1482-3
© 2015 Shell Educational Publishing, Inc.

Writing Is Magic, Or Is It?

Table of Contents

Foreword

'Writing is magic, as much the water of life as any other creative art.

The water is free. So drink. Drink and be filled up."

— Stephen King

Today, we know good teaching is rooted in research and practice. We know that our students, as writers, follow varied paths. As teachers, we need to know where to meet them on their path to chaperone them through their journey. *Writing Is Magic, Or Is It?* facilitates the process from student to teacher and back to student. This unique "zoom in, zoom out" approach makes this book relevant to every writing classroom today. Students need to see it, study it, and apply it.

This timely resource pairs everything we know about classic elements of good teaching with the modern-day demand of rigorous standards. Using mentor texts to study genre content and author's craft is a foundational way of showing students what good writing looks like. However, the brilliancy of the content design is in the approach of each genre. Students close read a mentor text and are taught various elements of the author's craft in that mentor text.

Specifically, students engage in a close read of each mentor text to not only shape their own ideas about the genre but to highlight the author's craft elements firsthand. They jot their notes directly onto the mentor text. Samples of these "jottings" are included with each mentor text. The teacher then guides students to deeper levels of understanding about the writer's craft before releasing students to create their own original piece. This authentic and holistic approach to genre writing sets the student up successfully with practical and important lessons. They are illustrative in nature for maximum benefits with instruction, yet demanding and complex enough to make a real difference in the development of student writing.

The benefit for teachers using this resource comes in the planning. Teachers have 18 mentor texts and multiple mini lessons at their fingertips. This enables them to meet their students where they currently are as writers, at all levels, and move them forward.

Likewise, the benefits for students are far reaching. They will not just be told what to do but shown how to do it. They will be provided a model, while being guided through the critical process of thinking and structuring the thinking to creating a piece of writing.

This resource leaves no stone unturned, as it will take a teacher through the process of writing in each genre. While there is a straightforward approach to teaching the author's craft with foundational skills explained for novice or experienced teachers, there are also new, fresh ideas on mini-lessons (referred to as Genre Specific writing strategies). A few great ones include a writing strategy for narrative fiction with creating a Thoughtshot (stopping the action for deep description), writing circular endings (start and end similarly to highlight or show evolution of a piece of text), and writing leads and endings specifically for non-fiction text. These will give any writing classroom structure and cultivate creativity as the strategies work well for all kinds of learning modalities.

Zoom in and teach, then zoom out and enjoy the magic you will see happen in your students' writing.

-Melissa Cheesman Smith, M.Ed.

Dedications

To my mom and dad. You both continue to inspire me. *JMB*

To Connor, who fills our lives with magical moments. *MCM*

Chapter 1

Writers As Writers (and Readers)

Many young—and not-so-young writers—think that writing is magical. Good writers, some believe, have captivating ideas at their fingertips, jot down what they are thinking, and immediately produce a perfect text, like magic. We know, however, that this is seldom the case. Donald Murray once wrote, "Writing is a craft before it is an art; writing may appear magic, but it is our responsibility to take our students backstage to watch the pigeons being tucked up the magician's sleeve" (1985, 4).

In *Writing Is Magic, Or Is It?*, we attempt to reveal how pigeons get tucked up magicians' sleeves. We analyze the writing of several children's authors, looking closely at how each author crafted his or her text. After analyzing each text, we identify writing strategies the author used, give each strategy a name, provide lesson ideas, and invite teachers and students to try out the strategies.

Throughout the book, we investigate aspects of craft that contribute to effective writing, such as leads, conclusions, voice, point of view, line breaks, sentence construction, and the use of grammar and mechanics to convey meaning. Our goal is to help students read as writers—to apprentice themselves with accomplished writers who can serve as auxiliary teachers.

Before we dive deeply into the classroom-based genre chapters that follow, we set a context in this chapter for what is to come. We look briefly at what research says about writing and writers, review the elements of the writing process, and take a peek at the processes used by some notable children's authors. Finally, with the Common Core State Standards (National Governors Association and Council of Chief State School Officers 2010a) in mind, we zoom in on the reading-writing connection, acknowledging the impact that close reading has in revealing both what accomplished writers say, as well as how they craft their messages.

Writing as a Process

Writing Anchor Standard 5 of the English Language Arts Common Core State Standards expects students to "Develop and strengthen writing as needed by planning, revising, editing, rewriting, or trying a new approach." In other words, writers engage in a process. Although the Introduction to the Standards (2010) explicitly states that the document does not mandate any particular writing process, it is likely that most teachers and students will use the popular Flower and Hayes (1981) model; therefore, let us begin by reviewing the components of this recursive writing process.

Planning

Planning is a key component of writing. According to Linda Flower and John R. Hayes (1981), planning involves generating ideas, organizing or giving structure to ideas, and setting goals. Many students we have worked with find it difficult to generate ideas. They have the impression that good topics must involve life-altering experiences. Yet authors regularly write about people, places, and events they know. E. L. Konigsburg, author of the 1968 Newbery Medal Award for *From the Mixed-Up Files of Mrs. Basil E. Frankweiler*, for example, gets her ideas "from things I've read, people I've met, situations I know about" (E. L. Konigsburg Interview Transcript, para. 6). She reports that in all her books, even in her historical fiction, the characters are drawn from people she knows. She offers a tip for writers, suggesting that they take everyday events and ask "what if?" to generate fresh, new ideas (E. L. Konigsburg Interview Transcript, para. 6). Interestingly, when asked where he gets his ideas, Jack Gantos, author of many books including the *Rotten Ralph* series and *Joey Pigza*, explains that for inspiration, he often mines journals he kept as a child. From his journals, he pulls ideas about his in- and out-of-school adventures, his friends, and his family. Although his own youth serves as inspiration for much of his writing, he also relies on current experiences. The main character in *Joey Pigza*, for instance, was based on a real-life boy he met while visiting a school in Pennsylvania (Biography—Jack Gantos, paras. 4 and 5).

As previously noted, in many cases, writers recast everyday experiences into interesting texts for readers. The same is true for Laurence Yep, author of *Dragonwings* and several other books. In an interview, Yep said "good writing brings out what's special in ordinary things. So all you really need is a brother—I actually wrote a book about the time I gave my brother a pet alligator. But really, writing only requires taking one step to the side and looking at something from a slightly different angle. So you can find unicorns in the garden, and monsters sitting next to you" (Laurence Yep Interview Transcript, para. 2).

Far less frequently, ideas just appear. J. K. Rowling disclosed that she was on a long train ride from Manchester to London, England, and the idea for the Harry Potter series "just fell into my head. At that point it was essentially the idea for a boy who didn't know he was a wizard, and the wizard school he ended up going to" (Harry Potter Lexicon: "About the Harry Potter Books: In Rowling's Own Words," para. 1).

Translating

Once writers generate an idea (or ideas), they translate their thoughts into words. Flower and Hayes (1981) define "translating" as "putting ideas into visible language" (373). Unlike magic tricks, however, in which magicians must follow a carefully scripted set of procedures to create a successful illusion, writers follow varied paths when moving from what is in their heads to coherent written messages for readers. Over the years, we have worked with some students who seem to write fluently most of the time, especially if writing within a genre or about a topic they know well. Other students, despite the genre or their background knowledge, struggle to get their ideas down on paper. The source of the challenge may reside in their planning.

Consider these planning questions:

- Did they keep a systematic list of possible topics or mine their writer's notebooks for ideas before writing?
- Did they take time to plan by thinking, writing, drawing, or talking about their ideas? If so, did they develop a plan that was adequate to get them started?
- Did they over-plan and lock themselves into an inflexible draft?
- Did they refer back to their plans or ignore them when translating?

Of course, the source of the problem may also reside in a student's knowledge of his or her topic, purpose, audience, or genre; or perhaps even in the quality of strategies and tools he or she is using (or not using), such as a pen, computer, tablet, or audio recorder, to translate abstract ideas into concrete words.

Despite having effective plans, knowledge, strategies, and tools, translating can be challenging. Accomplished authors, such as Cynthia Voigt, author of the *Mister Max* series among other titles, admit to sometimes having trouble starting to express ideas in written language (Cynthia Voigt Interview Transcript, para. 7). Perhaps the challenge can be attributed, in part, to the fact that there is no one, right formula to rely on when moving from an idea to an initial draft. Authors use different approaches to initiate the process of getting their ideas from their heads to paper. (See Figure 1)

Figure 1: Author Approaches to Writing

Writer	Processes for Translating Ideas	Reference
David Adler	Creates outlines.	David Adler Interview Transcript, para. 11
Cynthia Voigt	Creates outlines.	Cynthia Voigt Interview Transcript, para. 19
Chris Van Allsburg	Brainstorms at night in bed before he falls asleep. Creates outlines.	Chris Van Allsburg Interview Transcript, para. 9
Judy Blume	Uses a notebook. Determines where to begin and where she might end the story.	Judy Blume – Interview with Cynthia Leitich Smith, 4th section of the interview.
Walter Dean Myers	Uses detailed storylines to help shape his initial thinking.	Walter Dean Myers Interview Transcript, para. 4

Here are excerpts from interviews with three children's authors to illustrate how complex and unique the process of capturing and recording ideas can be. In a PBS

(Public Broadcasting System) interview, Shannon Hale, New York Times best-selling author of six young adult novels, including *Princess Academy*, explains that she begins by laying down "a skeleton" of her story, basically a chronological list of events. She does not worry about her characters until after she has the events in place so the characters can develop within the events she creates (Shannon Hale, slide 4).

In contrast to Hale's focus on events, Sid Fleischman, author of *Bull Run* among others, notes that he begins with a few characters around which interesting conflicts or a story may grow (Transcript from an Interview with Sid Fleischman, "The Process" section).

Different still is the process of Phyllis Reynolds Naylor, author of *Shiloh*. She compares her first draft to a director's first rehearsal: "you're just talking about who comes in where and who goes out..." She often scribbles the frame of her first thoughts on a clipboard, and continues to refine her work in her second draft. She claims to love writing third drafts because the story is underway, and it is then that she can begin to "tinker with it" (Transcript from an Interview with Phyllis Reynolds Naylor, "The Third Draft" section).

Revising

This "tinkering" is what most of us refer to as revising. According to Kate Messner (2011), "Revision involves rethinking not what a piece of writing is, but what it might become" (3). Messner (2011) also notes, "Revision is where stories start to sing. Where lumpy writing gets smoothed out and where good writing turns into great writing. It's the part where the real magic happens" (3).

It has been reported that Roald Dahl, a masterful writer, once said, "By the time I am nearing the end of a story, the first part will have been reread and altered and corrected at least one hundred and fifty times." Later he went on to say, "I am suspicious of both facility and speed. Good writing is essentially rewriting. I am positive of this" (approx. 1965, RD/6/2/1/23). Students may be fascinated to learn that it took Dahl three years to write *Charlie and the Chocolate Factory* (Roald Dahl Museum and Story Centre).

According to a document housed in the Roald Dahl Museum and Story Centre, Dahl began work on the manuscript sometime in 1961 and completed it in 1964 (dates are approximate). In early drafts, Dahl hid ten Golden Tickets each week. The number soon changed from ten to seven weekly tickets, and after several revisions, seven golden tickets in total were issued. Dahl changed character names, too (e.g., Violet Strabismus became Violet Beauregarde), and several characters who appeared in earlier drafts never made it to the five children in the final publication. Other changes, such as the addition of Charlie's grandparents in a 1962 draft, illustrate how the story evolved as Dahl shaped and reshaped it. (For early drafts of *Charlie and the Chocolate Factory*, see http://www.roalddahlmuseum.org/discoverdahl/index.aspx.) Few students seem to like to revise. Most interpret the revision process as being fairly linear, with revision and editing relegated to the final "stages" of the process, when all that is left to do is to fix up minor flaws. We learn from Roald Dahl, however, that revision is ongoing and that the entire text—from characters, to plot, to resolutions—can be altered by revision decisions an author makes throughout the process.

When asked what advice he had for young writers, Ridley Pearson, author of *The Kingdom Keepers* series responded: "Your writing is never good enough the first time. You're too close to it. You're too involved with it. You need to go back and put in better verbs and take out the *was's* and *is's*. You need to shorten things. You need to move this idea to the front. Just keep reworking your material" ("Writers Speak to Kids: Ridley Pearson," 4th question). We agree with Ridley Pearson's advice because he speaks to both the content and mechanics of writing; yet, many students may need guidance before they can independently make the local and global changes Pearson refers to in his interview. According to Carole Beal (1996), even when third and fifth graders went back to revise, many found it difficult to put themselves in the place of a reader, to evaluate the "communicative quality" of a text and to diagnose the specific types of problems that needed revision (e.g., where there are inconsistencies), especially when they did not have a great deal of content knowledge about their topic.

As teachers, we can show students how to detect, diagnose, and revise weak texts across genres, tasks, purposes, and audiences as initial steps taking them "backstage to watch the pigeons being tucked up the magician's sleeve" (Murray 1985, 4). In doing so, we are preparing them to successfully meet Writing Anchor Standard 10 of the Common Core State Standards, which expects students to "Write routinely over extended time frames (time for research, reflection, and revision) and shorter time frames (a single sitting or a day or two) for a range of tasks, purposes, and audiences" (2010a).

Learning from Accomplished Writers

It is important to look at what we know about more accomplished writers versus writers who are on their way to becoming accomplished. If we know how students typically develop as writers and understand how accomplished writers craft meaningful texts, we may be in a position to close the gap between mature writers and those who have not yet reached proficiency.

According to Marlene Scardamalia and Carl Bereiter, novice writers tend to focus on what the researchers call a "take what comes next" strategy (1986, 68). That is, writers go from one sentence to the next by searching their memories, retrieving content, and then writing it down. They work through a piece thinking about "what's next?" rather than following a goal-driven, recursive process that expert writers use. Furthermore, Ted Sanders and Joost Schilperoord (2006) report that the texts of many novice writers appear to be a list of underdeveloped ideas that are connected to an overall topic, but not necessarily to each other. The ideas may appear to be placed randomly in the text because they are recorded in the order in which they are retrieved from memory. Mature writers, on the other hand, tend to develop themes and expand upon ideas. Rather than randomly placed, ideas are intentionally organized to help writers communicate meaning.

Additionally, research has shown that when revising, novice writers tend to view their writing as a series of parts rather than an integrated whole, and focus on local, surface aspects of writing rather than meaning (Flower et al. 1986; Sommers 1980). Less accomplished writers revise until they believe they have satisfied all the "rules" of writing (Sommers 1980), addressing aspects of writing such as spelling, mechanics, neatness, and word choice (Lin, Monroe, and Troia 2007). Experienced writers, on the other hand, more often are goal-directed, focus on audience, and tackle global aspects of writing (Flower et al. 1986; Sommers 1980). A study by Shin-Ju Lin, Brandon Moore, and Gary Troia (2007) revealed this same general pattern in the development of "typically-developing writers" in grades 2 through 8, who progressed from a local focus on product to a more global focus on process, audience, and the communication of ideas. "Struggling writers" in these same grades, however, continued to focus on mechanics and product over process.

The Reading-Writing Connection

One way to help students become more proficient writers is to encourage them to read not only as readers who attend to comprehension, but also as writers who take note of how and why authors make decisions about content and craft.

The National Council of Teachers of English (2004) states in its "Beliefs About the Teaching of Writing" that "People who read a lot have a much easier time getting better at writing. In order to write a particular kind of text, it helps if the writer has read that kind of text. In order to take on a particular style of language, the writer needs to have read that language, to have heard it in her mind, so that she can hear it again in order to compose it" (Reading and Writing Are Related section, para. 1).

Writers such as Jacqueline Woodson, author of *Locomotion*, and Julius Lester, author of *John Henry*, point to reading as a key component in their success as writers. In fact, Judy Schachner, author of the *Skippyjon Jones* books, acknowledges, "I have to say that everything I've learned about writing is from reading..." (NBCLearn: Schachner interview, last question).

For many years, researchers, writers, and teachers have supported the use of mentor texts—texts written by more accomplished writers—as a way to provide readers with models they can use to learn about writing (Fletcher and Portalupi 2007; Myhill and Jones 2007). Notably, *Writing Next* (Graham and Perin 2007), a comprehensive review of writing research and instructional recommendations, lists the study of models as one of its eleven "Elements of Effective Adolescent Writing Instruction." The researchers encourage students and teachers to read and critically analyze the elements of mentor texts so they can imitate in their own writing.

High school teacher Lisa Garrigues (2004) did just that with her juniors, who were reading Ernest Hemingway's short stories. During a five-week unit, students read closely to determine such elements as:

- the impact of varying sentence lengths;

- the importance of using a limited number of precise, carefully chosen words;

- the implicit understandings that remain beneath the surface of the writing;

- the use of dialogue to reveal—or not reveal—information; and

- the challenges involved in creating realistic characters.

Garrigues (2004) purposefully and systematically taught students how to apprentice themselves to authors from whom they learned the craft of writing.

Not all students are fortunate enough to have teachers who provide instruction that helps them develop as writers (Butler and Britt 2011) and who teach them how to "read the writer's craft" (Garrigues 2004). However, with the adoption of the Common Core State Standards, there is a renewed interest in the reading-writing connection. It is true that we expect to see writing and writers play a prominent role in the writing standards; yet, it may come as a surprise to see so many references to writing and writers front and center in the Common Core State Reading Anchor Standards (2010).

We have italicized the language in the following Reading Anchor Standards that emphasizes how and why writers craft texts for readers:

Key Ideas and Details

- CCSS.ELA-Literacy.CCRA.R.1 Read closely to determine what the text says explicitly and to make logical inferences from it; *cite specific textual evidence when writing* or speaking to support conclusions drawn from the text.

- CCSS.ELA-Literacy.CCRA.R.2 Determine central ideas or themes of a text and *analyze their development; summarize the key supporting details and ideas.*

- CCSS.ELA-Literacy.CCRA.R.3 *Analyze how and why individuals, events, or ideas develop and interact over the course of a text.*

Craft and Structure

- CCSS.ELA-Literacy.CCRA.R.4 Interpret words and phrases as they are used in a text, including determining technical, connotative, and figurative meanings, and *analyze how specific word choices shape meaning or tone.*

- CCSS.ELA-Literacy.CCRA.R.5 *Analyze the structure of texts, including how specific sentences, paragraphs, and larger portions of the text (e.g., a section, chapter, scene, or stanza) relate to each other and the whole.*

- CCSS.ELA-Literacy.CCRA.R.6 *Assess how point of view or purpose shapes the content and style of a text.*

Integration of Knowledge and Ideas

- CCSS.ELA-Literacy.CCRA.R.7 *Integrate and evaluate content* presented in diverse media and formats, including visually and quantitatively, as well as in words.

- CCSS.ELA-Literacy.CCRA.R.8 *Delineate and evaluate the argument and specific claims in a text, including the validity of the reasoning as well as the relevance and sufficiency of the evidence.*

- CCSS.ELA-Literacy.CCRA.R.9 *Analyze how two or more texts address similar themes or topics* in order to build knowledge or to compare the approaches the authors take.

The only reading standard that does not make an explicit connection between reader and writer is Reading Anchor Standard 10: CCSS.ELA-Literacy.CCRA.R.10 "Read and comprehend complex literary and informational texts independently and proficiently."

Timothy Shanahan, a proponent of close reading, recommends that students read complex texts three times: first to find out what the text says, second to find out how the text works, and finally to determine what the text means (2012a). According to Shanahan, "A second reading would, thus, focus on figuring out how this text worked. How did the author organize it? What literary devices were used and how effective were they? What was the quality of the evidence? If data were presented, how was that done? Why did the author choose this word or that word? Was the meaning of a key term consistent or did it change across the text?" (2012b, para. 3).

Because reading-writing interactions have long been shown to influence comprehension (and more recently, to affect writing), it seems reasonable to pay close attention to the writer's craft as part of the reading process. To prepare for close readings, teachers examine the text demands (i.e., things that make the text challenging to comprehend). They consider aspects such as author's purpose, text structure, literary devices, word choices/language, and cohesion (e.g., transitions, conjunctions).

As we conclude this chapter, we cannot help but wonder if Donald Murray had Sid Fleischman in mind when he wrote about writers, magicians, and pigeons (1985). Fleischman, author of *The Whipping Boy*, which earned the 1987 Newbery Award, was a skilled magician who traveled with a magic show as a young man. At 19, he published his first book about the magic tricks he invented. He was so excited to see his name on the book that he wrote four additional magic books. He gradually moved from writing books about magic tricks to stories with trick endings. In an interview, he explained, "And then I thought well, a mystery novel is just a magic trick, you know, how did the murderer get away with it, but the authors... they're nice people, they explain at the end, magicians are rats, they don't explain it, that was the only difference" (Transcript from an Interview with Sid Fleischman, "Nothing up My Sleeve" section).

About This Book: Content and Organization

In this practical, standards-based book, we dive deeply into multiple genres: poetry, narrative fiction, informative/explanatory, narrative nonfiction, and opinion/argument. Each chapter includes mentor texts that the teacher can read aloud (or have students read independently) to get a general idea of what the text says—a basic understanding of the author's message. Next, we discuss the close reading of the mentor texts, looking at features of content and craft such as how the author organized it, the literary devices used, why the author chose a particular word, the meaning of a key term and if it is used consistently across the text, how effective the leads are, how transitions and conclusions are constructed, tone, style (word choice and sentence construction), pacing, titles, and use of punctuation to convey meaning. For each text, we then provide a copy of our "jottings"—or annotations—to guide you through the close readings you will experience with students. Finally, after looking holistically at a text, we zoom in to make transparent specific writing strategies the authors used to create the texts. We explain and name the strategies so young writers use a common language when talking about writing with their peers and teachers. Finally, we zoom out, inviting students to apply the strategies in their own writing.

In the next chapter, we dive deeply into how magicians tuck pigeons up their sleeves as we explore narrative fiction.

Reflection Questions

1. How can the authors mentioned in this chapter, and those whose work you study, serve as mentors for the students in your class?

2. In what ways can the Common Core or your own state's standards guide you as you investigate how texts work?

Chapter 2

Narrative Fiction Writing

The late Donald Graves, an inspirational writing teacher and researcher, was fond of saying, "You have a story to tell" (National Council of Teachers of English [NCTE] 2013). These words come to mind as we consider the genre of narrative fiction writing.

> 'You have a story to tell' (NCTE 2013) is a powerful message for writers of all ages; storytelling is how we communicate our life experiences, how we connect with others, and how we think about our place in the world. In fact, students who gather family stories to tell in class create connections to their pasts and feel as though the knowledge they bring to school is just as important as the knowledge they learn from the teacher" (Hamilton and Weiss 2005).

The process of recording the stories we tell, whether they are true or imagined, is the essence of narrative fiction writing. The Common Core State Standards assert that, "narrative fiction writing conveys experience, either real or imaginary, and uses time as its deep structure" and that "it can be used for many purposes, such as to inform, instruct, persuade, or entertain" (Appendix A, 23).

While we all have a story to tell, we should keep in mind that "how writers write is a complex, at times even quirky, process filled with starts and stops and twists and turns of seemingly infinite variety" (Peha 2003, 4). You have probably experienced how "even writers themselves are often at a loss to explain exactly how they do what they do" and that "many might even say they do things a little differently every time they start a new project" (Peha 2003, 4). As Steve Peha reminds us, "that's just the truth of writing: there's no one best way to do it" (2003, 4).

We agree. We also believe that, for narrative writers and writers of all genres, the pigeons that are tucked up the sleeves of magicians are the writing strategies that we can name. Instead of asking students to "add more," we suggest, for example, that they try a circular ending or they add a metaphor. These are specific, named strategies that students can apply to their current piece of narrative fiction writing and also apply to future pieces of narrative fiction writing.

We believe that teaching students specific strategies will empower them with ways to "provide visual details of scenes, objects, or people; to depict specific actions (for example, movements, gestures, postures, and expressions); to use dialogue and interior monologue that provide insight into the narrator's and characters' personalities and motives; and to manipulate pace to highlight the significance of events and create tension and suspense" (CCSSO Appendix A, 23–24).

Let us begin our exploration of narrative fiction writing by looking at the skills and understandings identified in the English Language Arts Standards for Writing Informative/Explanatory Texts (CCSS 2010 available at http://www.corestandards.org/ ELA-Literacy/W/introduction). These standards reflect what students should know and be able to do by the end of the identified academic year. As you look horizontally across the rows in the following chart, you will find the skills and understandings associated with writing narrative texts in grades 3 through 8. Looking vertically down each column, you will see how each skill or understanding increases in complexity. Rather than rewrite the standard in each box, we have included only the changes/ additions from grade to grade, as reflected in the language that we have taken directly from the standards.

Grade	Skills and Understandings Students Must Demonstrate by the End of Each Grade					
	Introduce a Topic	Develop a Topic	Link Ideas/ Transitions	Precise language	Formal Style	Concluding Statement
Grade 3	Establish a situation and introduce a narrator and/or characters; organize an event sequence that unfolds naturally.	Use dialogue and descriptions of actions, thoughts, and feelings to develop experiences and events or show the response of characters to situations.	Use temporal words and phrases to signal event order.	N/A	N/A	Provide a sense of closure.
Grade 4	Orient the reader...	Use dialogue and description...	Use a variety of transitional words and phrases to manage the sequence of events.	Use concrete words and phrases and sensory details to convey experiences and events precisely.	N/A	Provide a conclusion that follows from the narrated experiences or events.

Grade	Skills and Understandings Students Must Demonstrate by the End of Each Grade					
	Introduce a Topic	Develop a Topic	Link Ideas/ Transitions	Precise language	Formal Style	Concluding Statement
Grade 5	...organize an event sequence that unfolds naturally.	Use narrative techniques, such as dialogue, description, and pacing, to develop experiences and events or show the responses of characters to situations.	...and clauses...	Same as Grade 4	N/A	Same as Grade 4
Grade 6	Engage and orient the reader by establishing a context... organize an event sequence that unfolds naturally and logically.	Use narrative techniques, such as dialogue, pacing, and description, to develop experiences, events, and/or characters.	...to convey sequence and signal shifts from one time frame or setting to another.	...relevant descriptive details, and sensory language...	N/A	Same as Grade 4
Grade 7	...and point of view...	Same as Grade 6	Same as Grade 6	...to capture the action...	N/A	...and reflects on the narrated experiences or events.
Grade 8	Same as Grade 7	...and reflection...	...and show the relationships among experiences and events.	Same as Grade 7	N/A	Same as Grade 7

Writing Strategies Used in Narrative Fiction Writing

The narrative pieces in this chapter model the use of specific craft strategies. Through close reading, we identify the following writing strategies, and we discuss how the writer uses strategies to communicate and enhance the meaning of the narratives.

Snapshot: When we use a camera, we take a snapshot to allow others to see exactly what we see. Writers can do this with words. A snapshot is a detailed physical description of what you want your reader to see in his or her mind (Lane 1993). For example, authors might write a snapshot to show the physical details of a character's expression, the physical details of a place, or the physical details of a building.

Simile: A simile is a figure of speech. The writer compares two things by using the word *like* or by using the word *as*. The purpose of a simile is to paint a clear picture in the reader's mind by drawing on something the reader likely knows. You might have heard the similes: *as cute as a button* or *eats like a bird*.

Thoughtshot: According to creator Barry Lane (1993), in order to create a thoughtshot, writers stop the action for a brief moment and reveal what a character is thinking or feeling. Thoughtshots allow the reader to hear the exact words that the character is thinking. Writers often signal the use of a thoughtshot with phrases including, *I thought to myself, I kept thinking, I said to myself,* or *I wondered*. The exact thoughts are written in quotations or in italics.

Flashback: Although some stories are written entirely in the form of a flashback, students can also insert a flashback that is a relatively quick moment in the writing piece, a paragraph or so, in which the character remembers something meaningful that happened in the past. According to Ralph Fletcher and JoAnn Portalupi, "glimpses into the past can be used to develop character, invite readers into significant moments gone by, or make contrasts that point to important changes that have occurred (2007, 113).

You will find a clean "student copy" of each mentor text in Appendix B. If you think your students will be able to understand, or at least get the gist of the text on their own, begin by providing them with copies of the text, have them read it independently (or with a partner), and annotate it as they read. In their jottings, they should note text features (e.g., italicized words, headings, and key words), interesting or unfamiliar use of language, the organizational structure of the text, questions the text raises for them, author's craft (e.g., alliteration, metaphor, varied sentence constructions, effective leads, transitions, and conclusions). If you think the text may be too challenging for your students to comprehend independently, distribute the clean copy and then engage in a guided close read. (See the next two sections for guidance.)

Once students have read and annotated the text (i.e., completed their "jottings"), call them together into a large group to discuss the content of the text (i.e., *What* does the text say?) and then to investigate how the author crafted the text (i.e., *How* does the text say it?). Rather than share our sample jottings directly with your students, we envision that you will use our annotations to help guide your students through the close readings.

Transitional Phrases to Signal a Flashback: Flashbacks are often signaled with phrases that ease transition for readers such as *I remember one time when, I remembered back to the time when, Once when I was,* or *My mind traveled back to when.*

Flash-Forward: In order to provide readers with a glimpse into the future, writers can stop the chronological sequence of events in a piece of writing and transition to a flash-forward. In a flash-forward, the character or narrator imagines a key event that could happen but has not yet happened. A flash-forward can be as short as a couple of sentences. These meaningful scenes are often signaled by phrases that ease the transition for readers such as *I imagined myself..., I began to think about...,* or *My mind drifted to the future...*

AAAWWUBBIS Words (After, Although, As, When, While, Until, Because, Before, If, Since): AAAWWUBBIS serves as a mnemonic device for recalling subordinating conjunctions. A subordinating conjunction allows the dependent clause to join the main clause in order to express meaning. (*After we walk on the beach, we will get an ice cream.*) When a sentence begins with an AAAWWUBBIS word, writers usually need to use a comma after the opening phrase (unless the main clause is very short). Writers can use AAAWWUBBIS words to create sentence variety.

In addition to the word *although*, the words *even though* and *though* also count as AAAWWUBBIS words, and in addition to the word *when*, the word *whenever* counts (Anderson 2005).

Dialogue and Dialogue Tags: Dialogue can be used to move the story along, to control the pacing, to reveal character's motivations, and to reveal a relationship among characters. Dialogue tags are also used to express a character's feelings or intent. For example, the dialogue tag, "with tears in her eyes" shows that the character does not want to leave her dog in the following sentence: *"I hope to see you soon, Frank,"* whispered Lucy with tears in her eyes.*

Emotional ending: When a writer decides to write a story that shows strong emotion, it can be powerful to match the ending to the emotion conveyed throughout the story (Fletcher and Portalupi 2007).

Mentor Text (Fiction): Excerpt from "Giving Back"

(See Appendix B for Complete Text)

GIVING BACK

By Jenn Bogard

Edwin zig-zagged through the boundary of beach grass that separated his great-grandfather's old boat shop from the busy freeway. The shop was sheltered by weathered shingles—mostly yellow in color, yet the grays and greens of past generations peeked through. Edwin clasped the handle of the raw, splintered door bitten by years of icy winds and salty sprays. He creaked the door open and peered inside.

The shelves were still lined with gallons of resin and gallons of paint. Resting on the floor was an old cardboard box filled with sketches and secrets of boat building. As Edwin closed his eyes, he remembered thinly sliced curls of wood spiraling to the wide pine floor like pinwheels turning in a summer breeze. "The shop is just the way great-grandpa left it," he thought to himself.

Additional Thoughts:
What do you wonder? What did you discover? What do you want to discuss?

Sample Jottings: Excerpt from "Giving Back"

Mentor Text (Fiction): Excerpt from "Giving Back"

(See Appendix B for Complete Text)

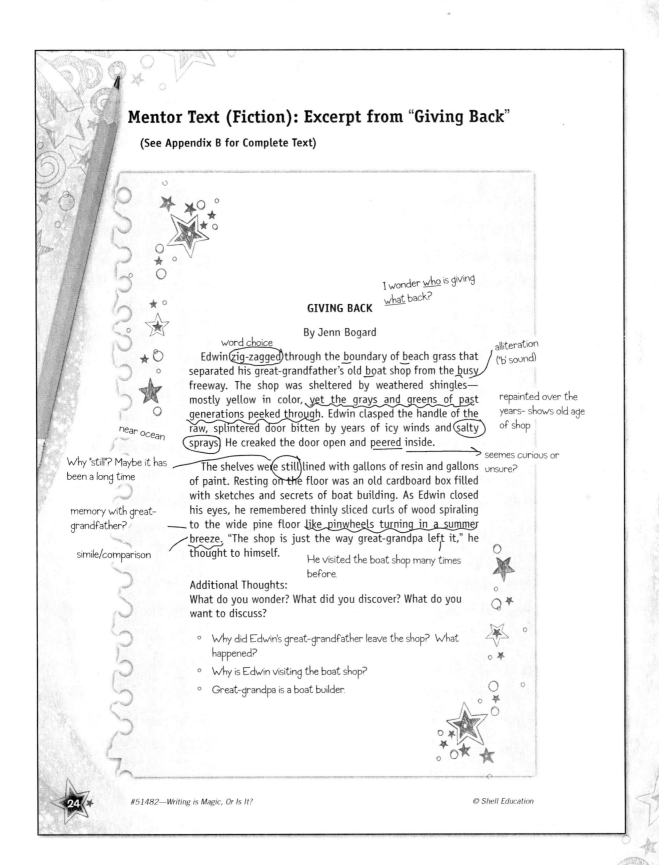

I wonder who is giving what back?

GIVING BACK

By Jenn Bogard

word choice

Edwin (zig-zagged) through the boundary of beach grass that separated his great-grandfather's old boat shop from the busy freeway. The shop was sheltered by weathered shingles—mostly yellow in color, yet the grays and greens of past generations peeked through. Edwin clasped the handle of the raw, splintered door bitten by years of icy winds and (salty sprays) He creaked the door open and peered inside.

alliteration ("b" sound)

repainted over the years- shows old age of shop

near ocean

seemes curious or unsure?

Why "still"? Maybe it has been a long time

The shelves were (still) lined with gallons of resin and gallons of paint. Resting on the floor was an old cardboard box filled with sketches and secrets of boat building. As Edwin closed his eyes, he remembered thinly sliced curls of wood spiraling to the wide pine floor like pinwheels turning in a summer breeze. "The shop is just the way great-grandpa left it," he thought to himself.

memory with great-grandfather?

simile/comparison

He visited the boat shop many times before.

Additional Thoughts:
What do you wonder? What did you discover? What do you want to discuss?

- Why did Edwin's great-grandfather leave the shop? What happened?
- Why is Edwin visiting the boat shop?
- Great-grandpa is a boat builder.

Close Reading: Excerpt from "Giving Back"

💬 What does the text say?

The purpose of this section is to address students' comprehension and to focus on what the text says. Here, we model how to ask text-dependent questions in order to allow students to infer meaning.

> **Close reading** is "an instructional routine in which students critically examine a text, especially through repeated readings" (Fisher and Frey 2012, 179). Using a short passage, students read carefully to determine what the text says and to uncover specific instances of the author's craft, including items such as word choice, sentence structure, endings, leads, and more.

1. Begin by asking students to share what they noticed: What did you jot down? What strikes you? What surprises you?

2. Guide students in figuring out what the text is saying. Have students retell what is happening in the passage. For example, students might say: Edwin visits his great-grandfather's abandoned boat shop. He finds that the shop is set up just as his great-grandfather left it. He recalls a memory of seeing slices of wood spiral to the floor.

   - Ask: Who is the main character? What is Edwin doing? Point out how Edwin "zig-zagged" to his great-grandfather's boat shop. Discuss the meaning of the word "zig-zagged," and ask students to describe the mental image they see when they hear the word.

   - Ask students to consider the mood of this first sentence. They will likely find the mood to be carefree.

   - Ask: What is a boat shop? What does this tell us about Edwin's great-grandfather? Discuss how he might be a boat builder for work or for a hobby.

3. Ask students to explain the meaning of the word "boundary," and, how the beach grass is a boundary that separates the boat shop from the freeway.

4. Ask for key details about the appearance of the boat shop: What does the boat shop look like? What color is the boat shop? Is it more than one color? How do you know? Have students figure out what the author means when she writes that the colors of the past generations "peeked through." What is the meaning of the word "generation"? What does the author mean when she writes that the colors "peeked" through?

5. Draw students to the phrase, "sheltered by weathered shingles." Ask students: How would the shop be sheltered? How would weathered shingles shelter the shop? What does "sheltered" mean? What does "weathered" mean?

6. What do you think the appearance of the boat shop tells us? Discuss how the shop has been repainted over the years and how the appearance shows the passage of time. Students might also infer that the shop has been neglected.

7. Invite students to locate additional details in the first paragraph that show the condition of the boat shop. Discuss how the door is "raw" and "splintered." What material is the door likely made of? What caused the door to splinter and to appear raw? Draw students to the phrase, "salty sprays." After giving students a

chance to figure out what a salty spray could be and what might cause a salty spray, discuss how this signifies close proximity to the salty ocean.

8. Have students share what they think is happening at the end of the first paragraph. Why do you think Edwin is peering inside as opposed to just heading right in?

9. Invite students to reread the second paragraph. Ask: What is happening now? Ask: What do we know about the inside of the boat shop? Direct students to notice the word, "still" in the first line. Ask: What do you think the author wants us to know when she writes, "The shelves were *still* lined..." Students might infer that Edwin has not been to the boat shop for some time and that he is comparing how the shop looks to how he remembers it.

10. Ask students to infer the meaning of the word *resin* and discuss how it might be a substance used in the boat building process.

11. Direct students to the phrase, "secrets of boat building." Ask them to infer what the author might mean when she writes that the box is filled with "sketches and secrets of boat building." Students might infer that the sketches and plans are like secrets because they show how the boat is made or that they unlock the mystery of how the boat is made by detailing the specific measurements and directions.

12. Ask students to explain what Edwin is remembering in the second paragraph. What are "thinly sliced curls of wood spiraling to the wide pine floor"? Students might not have knowledge of a wood planer, yet they might infer that the great-grandfather used some type of woodworking tool to shave and shape the wood in order to craft the boat.

13. Have students infer what is happening to the wood when it is *spiraling*. Ask: What does the author compare the spiraling curls of wood to? Discuss the meaning of the word *pinwheels*. Why do you think she compares the falling wood to turning pinwheels? What image does this create in your mind? Is the wood falling slowly or quickly? How do you know? Point out the phrase *summer breeze*. Ask students to describe a summer breeze. Discuss the peaceful, joyful mood of this image.

14. Finally, ask the students what they learn in the last sentence of the second paragraph. What does Edwin think to himself? How do you think Edwin feels about the shop being, "just the way great-grandpa left it"? Why do you think that? Gather students' thoughts about why Edwin's great-grandfather might have left the boat shop and when. Invite them to infer why Edwin is returning to the boat shop and how long it might have been since he last visited. Encourage students to use evidence from the text to support their inferences.

How does the text say it?

Here is the part when you invite students to reveal the pigeons tucked up the magician's sleeve. The intent of this section is to talk through *how* the text says what it says and to investigate the choices the author makes to reveal meaning. Discussion should involve literary devices, organization, and specific word choices.

1. Invite students to reread the first sentence, and remind them of the discussion you had about mood. Ask: How did the writer create the carefree mood of the first sentence? Draw students to notice the specific word choice, "zig-zagged." Have students read the first sentence aloud. Ask: How does the sentence sound when read aloud? Students might notice the smooth flow of the lengthy sentence that adds to the mood.

   • Ask: What other choices did the writer make in this sentence? Students might point out the repetition of the beginning sound of */b/* in the words *boundary*, *beach*, *boat*, and *busy*. Ask them if they think the writer's use of this alliteration adds to the mood and helps establish the tone of the scene for readers. Discuss how this lead includes action and shows what Edwin is doing.

2. Remind students about their discussion of the condition of the outside of the boat shop and how the shop has stood for generations. They most likely agreed that the shop is tattered.

   • Ask: How did the writer show us the condition and age of the shop? Did she come right out and say that the shop was tattered? Have students reread the following sentence, "The shop was sheltered by weathered shingles—mostly yellow in color, yet the grays and greens of past generations peeked through." Ask: What choices did the writer make in this sentence?

   • Discuss how the writer used words to create a detailed description so that we know exactly what the shop looked like. Tell students that a detailed description of what something or someone looks like is called a *snapshot*.

3. Invite students to reread the remainder of the excerpt to search for another snapshot.

   • Students will likely find the following snapshot: "The shelves were still lined with gallons of resin and gallons of paint. Resting on the floor was an old cardboard box filled with sketches and secrets of boat building."

   • Tell students to think about why the writer used this snapshot. Ask: Why didn't the writer just say that the shop was filled with boat building supplies?

   • Discuss how the snapshot allows us to know exactly what the main character sees. Ask students to consider how this physical description of the materials in the shop reveals clues about the characters. For example, students might infer that the great-grandfather works in the shop to build boats using sketches and plans.

4. Draw students' attention to the author's choice of the word, *still* in the first sentence of the second paragraph. Why would the writer use the word *still*? What was she up to? Students might decide that the word choice, is a way to let her readers know that time has passed since Edwin had last visited the boat shop.

5. Invite students to find additional places in the excerpt in which the writer made careful decisions about word choices. Students might locate the phrase, *salty sprays*. Discuss how this precise word choice allows the reader to infer the location of the boat shop—by the salty ocean.

6. Students might also note the strong verb of *peered* and how it shows the reader that Edwin is curious or tentative after opening the door to the boat shop, as if he did not know what to expect.

7. Draw students to the specific word choice of *secrets* and how the box was, "filled with sketches and secrets of boat building." Ask students to think about why the writer would choose to use the word *secrets*.

8. Have students reread the sentence: *As Edwin closed his eyes, he remembered thinly sliced curls of wood spiraling to the wide pine floor like pinwheels turning in a summer breeze.* Invite students to discuss: What is the author up to when she has Edwin remember back to this moment in his past? What is she revealing?

   • Discuss how the author uses a *flashback* to transition from the chronological sequence of the story to reveal how Edwin might have taken part in the boat-building process with his great-grandpa. Students might infer that he watched his great-grandpa shape the wood or that he helped his great-grandpa shape the wood.

9. Draw students' attention to the author's use of a simile in which she compares the spiraling curls of wood to "pinwheels turning in a summer breeze." Discuss how this comparison may or may not make the scene more vivid for the reader. Ask students to share their opinions of the effectiveness of this simile.

10. Finally, the excerpt ends with the sentence: *"The shop is just the way great-grandpa left it,"* he thought to himself. Invite readers to infer why the author includes Edwin's exact thoughts. Ask students: What does the author reveal by showing exactly what Edwin was thinking? How does this thought show that it is significant to Edwin that the shop is the same?

11. Tell students that this technique of revealing the character's exact thoughts is called a *thoughtshot*. Invite students to discuss: How effective is this thoughtshot? Does it reveal his relationship with his great-grandpa? Do we know how Edwin feels about the shop being the same? Have students suggest how they might add to this thoughtshot to reveal additional meaning to the reader.

Zooming In: Analyzing Writing Strategies

Here are four strategies that the author uses that you can also implement with students using the suggested lesson ideas that follow.

1. **Snapshot:** The author uses the following snapshot to allow readers to create a mental image and picture precisely what the main character sees in the boat shop: *The shelves were still lined with gallons of resin and gallons of paint. Resting on the floor was an old cardboard box filled with sketches and secrets of boat building.*

2. **Simile:** The use of a simile helps set the tone and create the main character's pleasant, heartwarming memory. For example, *a summer breeze evokes pleasant feelings of comfort.* The author compares the curls of wood to pinwheels turning in a summer breeze.

3. **Thoughtshot:** The action is stopped for a brief moment in order for Edwin to reveal his exact thoughts to the reader about his impression of seeing the shop after not having seen it for some time. The following thoughtshot allows readers to get inside Edwin's head and to hear his exact words *"The shop is just the way great-grandpa left it," he thought to himself.*

4. **Flashback:** The author transitions from the chronological sequence of events to a past event as Edwin remembers an experience at the boat shop. This short flashback allows the reader to infer that he spent time with is great-grandpa. The author writes: *As Edwin closed his eyes, he remembered his thinly sliced curls of wood spiraling to the wide pine floor like pinwheels turning in a summer breeze.*

Lesson Ideas: Excerpt from "Giving Back"

Once you and your students have identified instances of author's craft, we believe it is important to name the strategies and to empower students to try out the strategies in their own writing. These lesson ideas provide you with opportunities for your students to practice the strategies with support from you and their peers.

Snapshot

Discuss with students how we can use a camera to capture a photograph, or a snapshot, that shows others exactly what we saw. Explain that writers can do this with words. When writers create a detailed description of what they want their readers to *see* in their minds, we call that a snapshot.

1. Locate a snapshot in a book. Have students notice how the author creates a picture in the reader's mind as you read the snapshot aloud.

2. Bring in a physical object, such as funky sunglasses, an interesting hat, or a blooming plant. Guide students in writing a snapshot of the object, making sure that they describe, in detail, what they see.

3. Invite students to reread one of their own writing pieces. Have them reread for the intent of locating a spot where the reader might have difficulty picturing the story. Ask students to write a snapshot.

You might also model the use of a snapshot with **shared writing** by having the students help you add a snapshot to your own draft.

1. Write a short story or use the story below entitled, "Sixth Grade Camp."

   Sixth Grade Camp

   "I can't believe we were put into the birdwatching group," I whined to my friend, Rob. We were walking through the forest with binoculars hanging around our necks.

   "Ya, we're not going to see anything," Rob grumbled.

   Once we got to a clearing in the woods, I held the binoculars up to my eyes. I waited. I scanned the trees. I saw something.

   "It's a bird," I whispered with excitement. The binoculars let me see it up close.

   Suddenly, being picked for the birdwatching group didn't seem so bad.

2. Ask students to flag a spot in which a snapshot is needed to allow readers to visualize an important part. Discuss with students how the reader does not know what the bird looks like.

3. Ask students to find the specific place in the text where the snapshot could be added. Students might suggest adding the snapshot right after the sentence, *The binoculars let me see it up close.*

4. Discuss with students how there is no room to add a snapshot within the text, so a revision symbol is needed. Model how to draw the symbol of a camera after the word *close* in the text. Model how to draw the same symbol at the end of the writing piece and how that will allow you to add a snapshot. As students read along and come to the symbol in the text, they will need to jump down to the second symbol in order to read the snapshot.

5. Together with the studnets, write a snapshot for the bird. Tell students that you have a photo of what the bird might have looked like. Show them a large picture of an interesting bird from a calendar or from an Internet site.

6. Invite students into shared writing in which they look at the picture of the bird and offer sentences to describe what the bird looks like. Together as a class, participate in **shared writing** and create a short paragraph that describes the bird.

7. Reread the short story, jumping down to read the snapshot of the bird when you come upon the symbol of the camera.

8. Discuss with students how the snapshot allows readers to create a picture of the bird in their minds.

In **shared writing**, the teacher and students come up with ideas for the story together. The teacher writes the story down as it unfolds.

The snapshot strategy can also be taught by starting with a vague statement.

1. Display the sentence: "The kids were having fun on the playground."

2. Discuss with students how this sentence does not show us exactly what the kids are doing on the playground or what they look like as they are having fun.

3. Invite students to grab their notebook and pencil. Take students to the playground to observe a recess time. Have them write a snapshot to describe to readers exactly what they see students doing on the playground. Is someone on the swings? Are there groups of kids laughing? What do their facial expressions look like?

4. When back in the classroom, have students share their snapshots and compare them to the vague statement, "The kids were having fun on the playground."

5. Ask students to consider how the snapshot allows readers to create a mental image in their minds.

6. Give small groups additional vague statements and invite them to write snapshots. Statements might include: *The tropical fish look pretty* or *The truck was very old*. When possible, provide students with a visual, a concrete object, or a chance to observe as they are learning to write snapshots.

7. Invite students to locate a place to add a snapshot in their own writing.

Simile

Pull out the simile used in the text excerpt and display it for students: *thinly sliced curls of wood spiraling to the wide pine floor like pinwheels turning in a summer breeze.* Tell students that they will have the chance to evaluate the effectiveness of similes in various writing pieces, starting with the aforementioned simile from the excerpt, "Giving Back."

1. Together as a group, complete the following chart:

Record the simile.	Is this a commonly used simile? Have you heard it before?	Explain what is being compared and why you think the author compares them.	What information does the reader need to know in order for the simile to make sense and to add meaning?	In your opinion, is the simile effective? Why or why not?

2. Invite partnerships to partake in a simile hunt. Provide a wide range of materials, including popular songs, poems, newspaper articles, and books. Have students complete the table for each simile they find, critically analyzing its effectiveness.

3. Once students have located a handful of similes, conduct a class discussion. Ask: Did you find any similes that you have heard before? Did you find any original similes? Did you find any similes that added detail and enhanced meaning?

4. Create a class chart entitled, "The Pitfalls of Using Similes." Encourage your class to think about what they should avoid when writing a simile. For example, writers might use too many similes in one piece, or they might compare two things without considering their audience and the background knowledge they might have.

5. Invite students to revisit their own work. Have them add a simile and then together with a peer, fill out the chart to think about how effective the simile might be for readers.

Thoughtshot

Have students experiment with the impact of thoughtshots by revising the thoughtshot in the excerpt, "Giving Back."

1. Tell students that, when writing a thoughtshot, the action is stopped for a brief moment in order to reveal exactly what a character is thinking. Explain how writers can use this strategy to reveal information about a character such as feelings, predictions, intentions, and plans, in addition to the character's relationship with another character.

2. Display the thoughtshot used in the previous excerpt: *The shop is just the way great-grandpa left it, he thought to himself.*

3. Point out how this thoughtshot provides the reader with Edwin's reaction to seeing the shop. Ask students to give their opinion: Does this thoughtshot provide you with enough information about his thoughts and feelings, or do you want more information?

4. Have students read the entire story (See Appendix D).

5. Invite students to go back and revise the thoughtshot to reveal more detail. For example, they might use Edwin's thoughts to reveal how long it has been since he visited the shop, his purpose for visiting, or why his great-grandfather is not there.

6. Challenge students to add a thoughtshot to a piece of their own writing.

Flashback

Teach students that it is important to be picky in deciding what information to reveal in a flashback and that a flashback is a chance to give important details and information. Encourage students to revise the flashback in order to allow readers to "meet" Edwin's great-grandpa.

1. Direct students back to the flashback in the excerpt: *As Edwin closed his eyes, he remembered thinly sliced curls of wood spiraling to the wide pine floor like pinwheels turning in a summer breeze.*

2. Explain to students that writers can use the flashback strategy to provide readers with details about important information from the past.

3. Have students critically analyze the flashback by considering the questions: Does the flashback show us how Edwin and his great-grandpa interacted? Can you picture what his great-grandpa looked like? Can you hear what the characters might have said to one another?

4. Guide students in rewriting the flashback in this excerpt so that readers can "meet" his great-grandpa, hearing what he might have said to Edwin in the moment and seeing what he might have looked like.

5. Invite students to work in partnerships to add a flashback to their own piece of writing. Have students decide the purpose of their flashback beforehand.

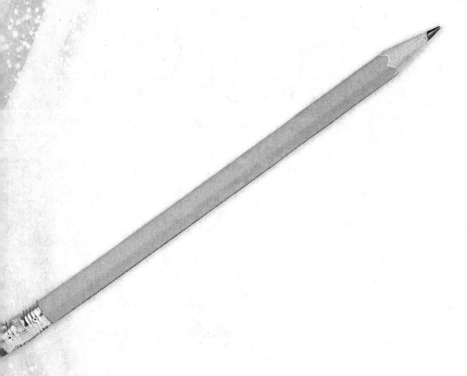

Mentor Text: Excerpt from "Sisters for Life"

(See Appendix D for Complete Text)

Sisters for Life

By Allie Piper

I curled up in Juliette's lap and hoped time would stop. We sat in silence, staring at the TV. I don't remember what we were watching, but it didn't matter because we weren't watching it anyway. We were just too sad to focus on anything.

My mind drifted back ten months to the very first time I met Juliette, our foreign exchange student who had come all the way from France. I remembered how my heart was beating like a hummingbird's wings as we drove to the hotel to pick her up. I remembered the questions that raced through my mind, "Will she like me?" "Will this be awkward?" "How will we communicate?" "Will we argue like real siblings?" I remembered seeing her chestnut-colored hair, her hazel eyes, and her bright smile with little braces on her teeth. There she was...my new 15-year-old sister, holding a small bag, a big bag, and handbag. I remembered how she gave me a big hug.

My mom interrupted my thoughts, "Kids, it's time for breakfast." But I didn't want it to be time for breakfast.

Sitting at the breakfast table with our five sad faces, it was different than our usual loud, laughing meals. Thinking about all of the travels, silliness, and fun we had together brought a smile to my face. A little giggle slipped out and I said, "I won't ever forget dancing in the elevator in California." Juliette laughed and replied, "or toilet paper volleyball!" Mom and Dad just looked confused because those were *our* secrets. James whined, "Dad, why does Juliette have to leave?"

Soon, the table became silent again. Juliette rested her fork on her plate and began to chew on her fingernails. As I stared at my half-eaten pancake, I imagined myself sitting in the window seat of a plane and hearing the pilot announce, "Welcome to France!" I imagined Juliette guiding me on my own tour of Paris, just like she promised. I imagined eating ham and cheese crepes with her, and I imagined taking the train from Paris to her house.

I leaned over and whispered, "Je t'aime" in Juliette's ear. Juliette hugged me and said, "Sisters for life." In that moment, I knew I would miss her, and I still miss her today.

Additional Thoughts:
What do you wonder? What did you discover? What do you want to discuss?

Sample Jottings: Excerpt from "Sisters for Life"

Mentor Text: Excerpt from "Sisters for Life"
(See Appendix D for Complete Text)

Sisters for Life

By Allie Piper

something great is coming to an end?

I curled up in Juliette's lap and <u>hoped time would stop</u>. We sat in silence, staring at the TV. I don't remember what we were watching, but it didn't matter because we weren't watching it anyway. We were just too sad to focus on anything.

simile

flashes back

My mind drifted back ten months to the very first time I met Juliette, our foreign exchange student who had come all the way from France. I remembered how my heart was beating like a hummingbird's wings as we drove to the hotel to pick her up. I remembered the questions that raced through my mind, "Will she like me?" "Will this be awkward?" "How will we communicate?" "Will we argue like real siblings?" I remembered seeing her chestnut-colored hair, her hazel eyes, and her bright smile with little braces on her teeth. There she was...my new 15-year-old sister, holding a small bag, a big bag, and handbag. I remembered how she gave me a big hug.

ends flashback

My mom interrupted my thoughts, "Kids, it's time for breakfast." But I didn't want it to be time for breakfast.

word choice

conversation shows relationship

specific times together

Sitting at the breakfast table with our five sad faces, it was different than our usual loud, laughing meals. Thinking about all of the travels, silliness, and fun we had together brought a smile to my face. A little giggle slipped out and I said, "I won't ever forget dancing in the elevator in California." Juliette laughed and replied, "or toilet paper volleyball!" Mom and Dad just looked confused because those were *our* secrets. James whined, "Dad, why does Juliette have to leave?"

flashes forward to the future

Soon, the table became silent again. Juliette rested her fork on her plate and began to chew on her fingernails. As I stared at my half-eaten pancake, I imagined myself sitting in the window seat of a plane and hearing the pilot announce, "Welcome to France!" I imagined Juliette guiding me on my own tour of Paris, just like she promised. I imagined eating ham and cheese crepes with her, and I imagined taking the train from Paris to her house.

What does this mean?

I leaned over and whispered, "Je t'aime" in Juliette's ear. Juliette hugged me and said, "Sisters for life." In that moment, I knew I would miss her, and I still miss her today.

emotional ending

Additional Thoughts:
What do you wonder? What did you discover? What do you want to discuss?

° Special relationship between narrator and Juliette

° Is this a memoir?

° Flashback and flash-forward reveal information

 #51482—Writing is Magic, Or Is It?   © Shell Education

Close Reading: Excerpt from "Sisters for Life"

💬 What does the text say?

The purpose of this section is to address students' comprehension and to focus on what the text says. Here, we model how to ask text-dependent questions in order to allow students to infer meaning.

Close reading is "an instructional routine in which students critically examine a text, especially through repeated readings" (Fisher and Frey 2012, 179). Using a short passage, students read carefully to determine what the text says and to uncover specific instances of the author's craft, including items such as word choice, sentence structure, endings, leads, and more.

1. Begin by asking students to share what they noticed *What did you jot down? What strikes you? What surprises you?*

2. Guide students in figuring out what the text is saying. Ask them to retell the chronological structure of the events. Students will most likely respond with the following events: the main character is sitting with Juliette, her "sister" who is a foreign exchange student. She is sad for some reason. The narrator thinks back to when she first met Juliette, including the worries she had in her mind and what Juliette looked like when she first saw her. The narrator's mother calls the family to breakfast. At breakfast, she and Juliette talk about the fun times they have experienced together. The narrator imagines the future. She imagines visiting Juliette in France and the things they will do together.

3. Ask: What is the narrator's name, and how do you know? Who are the other characters in the story? Do we know who James is, or do we have to infer it?

4. Invite students to describe the setting of the story. Discuss how the story begins in a room in the home with a TV and how the rest of the story takes place at the breakfast table. Ask students to explain the time frame of this story. Guide students to understand that, even though the narrator thinks back to meeting Juliette and later thinks ahead to visiting Juliette in France, the time span of this story is short—just the moments before breakfast and during breakfast. Ask students to estimate about how many minutes this entire story spans. Students might infer 30 minutes or an hour.

5. Ask students to find evidence in the text that reveals who Juliette is. Students will likely find the phrase: *our foreign exchange student who had come all the way from France.* Make sure that students know the meaning of the term *foreign exchange student.* Ask: What context clues reveal the meaning of this phrase?

6. Ask: What is the problem in this story? Discuss with students how the narrator's "sister," who is a foreign exchange student, is leaving. Ask students to find evidence in the text to explain how they know that this is the problem. Students might point out the last line of the text: *In that moment, I knew I would miss her, and I still miss her today.* Students might also locate places in the text that show how the narrator is feeling. Students might find the sentence: *Sitting at the breakfast table with our five sad faces, it was different than our usual loud, laughing meals.*

7. Ask: How does the narrator react to Juliette's leaving? Invite students to locate evidence in the text that show the narrator's emotions. Ask: How is Juliette feeling? How do you know? How is James feeling? How do you know?

8. Draw students' attention to the second paragraph that begins: *My mind drifted back ten months...* Ask them to explain what is happening. Discuss with students how the narrator is flashing back to the very first time she met Juliette and how the entire paragraph shows details that already happened ten months ago. Have students explain what was going through the narrator's mind when she met Juliette. Ask students to describe Juliette.

9. Ask students to reread the fourth paragraph that begins, *Sitting at the breakfast table with our five sad faces...* Ask: Who do you think is sitting at the table? What do we learn from the conversation at the table? What special times did the narrator share with Juliette?

10. Invite students to reread the next paragraph that begins: *Soon, the table became silent again.* Ask them to explain what that means. What does it imply? Discuss the melancholy mood of the breakfast and why the characters feel sad.

11. Ask: What happens when Juliette is staring at her half-eaten pancake? What does she do? Be sure that students understand that the narrator begins to think about the future. Ask: How do we know that the narrator is flashing forward to the future? What does she hope to do when she visits Juliette in France?

12. Draw students' attention to the last paragraph. What does the narrator whisper in Juliette's ear? Have students infer the meaning of the French phrase *Je t'aime.* (*I love you.*) Ask: What context clues help you to infer the meaning? Ask students to explain how Juliette responds.

13. Have students describe the relationship of the narrator and Juliette. Reread the final line of the story and ask: What new information is revealed in the final sentence? Discuss how the reader is left with the idea that their relationship has continued to remain special because the narrator still misses Juliette.

14. Finally, ask: Does the main character change in the story? How? Have students locate evidence in the text to support their thoughts. Students might point out that the narrator is sad until she realizes she can visit Juliette. They might point out that, ten months ago, the narrator had worrisome questions racing through her mind about how the experience of having a foreign exchange "sister" would go, and now, ten months later, she has a loving, sisterly relationship with Juliette.

How does the text say it?

Here is the part when you invite students to reveal the pigeons tucked up the magician's sleeve. The intent of this section is to talk through *how* the text says what it says and to investigate the choices the author makes to reveal meaning. Discussion should involve literary devices, organization, and specific words choices.

1. Begin by asking: What was the author up to when she organized the chronological structure of this story? Why did she have the narrator think back to when she first met Juliette? Discuss how this glimpse into the past gives readers important background information and shows how the narrator's relationship with Juliette started.

   • Ask: What information do we learn when the narrator remembers this meaningful moment? How did the author use this flashback to develop the character of the narrator? How did she use the flashback to develop the character of Juliette?

2. Tell students the strategy of having a character remember back to an important moment is called a *flashback*. Ask: How did the author signal to her readers that the character was about to flash back to the past? Discuss how the author transitions to the flashback with the words, *My mind drifted back ten months to the very first time I met Juliette...* and how this alerts the reader that the character is about to think back to another time.

3. Invite students to notice how the author lets the reader know that the flashback has ended.

   • Discuss how the author uses dialogue to transition the reader back to the present moment by writing: *My mom interrupted my thoughts, "Kids, it's time for breakfast."* Ask students if they think dialogue is an effective way to end a flashback, and have them explain their thinking.

4. Encourage students to locate another place in the text in which the author steps out of the chronological sequence of the moment.

   • Discuss how the narrator begins to imagine visiting Juliette in France. Have students reread the part that begins: *As I stared at my half-eaten pancake, I imagined myself sitting in the window seat of a plane...* Tell students that this strategy of the character thinking into the future is called a *flash-forward*.

   • Ask: Why did the author choose to write a flash-forward? What information is revealed through this glimpse into the future? Discuss how this flash-forward shows the character's wishes and reveals the special relationship between she and Juliette.

5. Invite students to notice additional strategies the author uses to reveal a special relationship between the narrator and Juliette. Have students locate another place in the story where they get a sense of the special relationship. Students will likely locate the conversation at the breakfast table. Ask: What does this conversation reveal? Discuss how the author allows us to hear dialogue that tells us about specific experiences they have shared.

   Students might also point out the dialogue at the end of the story when the narrator whispers, *Je t'aime* and when Juliette responds, *"Sisters for life."* Discuss how the author chooses the dialogue carefully to show feelings and relationship.

6. Ask students to find additional examples of dialogue in the story and to consider the author's purpose of using it. Students might point out the sentence: *James whined, "Dad, why does Juliette have to leave?"* Discuss how dialogue is used to show James' emotions and to allow readers to infer that he, too, has a special relationship with Juliette. Direct students to locate a specific word choice in this dialogue that also helps to reveal his feelings: *whined*. Explain that by using what is called a dialogue tag, readers know *how* James said these words, revealing his emotion.

7. Ask: What comparisons does the author use in the text? Students will likely locate the simile the author uses: *my heart was beating like a hummingbird's wings*. Ask students to explain the meaning of this comparison. How does the comparison allow us to understand how she felt? Ask: Are there additional places that cause you to create a vivid image in your mind?

8. Have students reread the fifth paragraph that begins: *Soon, the table became silent again*. Tell students that they will reread for a specific purpose: to look at how the author constructs her sentences. Ask: Do the sentences begin differently or the same? Are the sentences short or complex? How does the author use punctuation in these sentences?

   - Point out the following complex sentence: *As I stared at my half-eaten pancake, I imagined myself sitting in the window seat of a plane and hearing the pilot announce, "Welcome to France!"* Discuss how the beginning of this sentence is an opener that requires the remainder of the sentence to make meaning. Point out the use of a comma to join the opener to the main clause.

9. Students might also notice the author's choice to repeat the words *I imagined* in the construction of sentences in this paragraph. Ask students to read aloud the sentences with this repeated phrase. Ask: How does the repeated phrase affect the flow of the reading?

10. Encourage students to locate other places in the story in which the author creates an interesting or complex sentence structure. Ask: What does the author do to create the complex sentence? How does the punctuation help to make the sentence complex?

11. Finally, ask students to locate words or phrases that cause them to feel emotion. Reread the ending. Ask students how the end makes them feel. Have them point out the specific words and phrases that the author uses to create this emotional effect for the reader.

   - Discuss: How does the emotion of this ending match the emotion of the story? Why do you think the author chose to leave the reader with this emotion? Students might point out that the reader is left with the same emotion that the narrator experienced during her last breakfast with Juliette as part of her family.

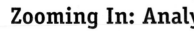

Zooming In: Analyzing Writing Strategies

Here are five strategies that the author uses that you can also implement with students using the suggested lesson ideas that follow.

1. **Transitional Phrases to Signal a Flashback:** The author stops the chronological sequence of events and has the narrator remember back to the very first time she met Juliette, providing readers with important background information and allowing them to fully experience the present story. Allie's flashback also develops the narrator's character by revealing the questions and worries that raced through her mind. Flashing back also helps to develop the character of Juliette because it shows her physical traits. The author signals the flashback with the phrase: *My mind drifted back ten months.*

2. **Flash-forward:** In order to provide readers with a glimpse into the future, the author stops the chronological sequence of the events during the breakfast and transitions to a flash-forward. The narrator imagines visiting Juliette in France and the specific experiences that they will share together once she is there. The author signals this meaningful scene by beginning her flash-forward with the phrase: *I imagined myself.*

3. **AAAWWUBBIS Words (After, Although, As, When, While, Until, Because, Before, If, Since):** The author creates variety in sentence structure, which allows for a smooth and interesting read. One way that she achieves this is by beginning sentences with AAAWWUBBIS words. She uses subordinating conjunctions to join the opener (dependent clause) with the main clause, and she uses a comma after the opening. For example, Allie uses an AAAWWUBBIS word in the following sentence: *As I stared at my half-eaten pancake, I imagined myself sitting in the window seat of a plane and hearing the pilot announce, "Welcome to France!"*

4. **Dialogue and Dialogue Tags:** The author uses dialogue to move the story along and to reveal the relationship between the narrator and Juliette. For example, the author writes: *A little giggle slipped out and I said, "I won't ever forget dancing in the elevator in California." Juliette laughed and replied, "or toilet paper volleyball!"*

   The author uses dialogue tags to express characters' feelings. For example, she uses the dialogue tag *whined* to show James' disappointment with Juliette having to leave: *James whined, "Dad, why does Juliette have to leave?"*

5. **Emotional ending:** The ending of the story leaves the reader with the feeling of sadness, which mirrors the overall sad emotion of the story. The author writes the following ending: *In that moment, I knew I would miss her, and I still miss her today.*

Lesson Ideas: Excerpt from "Sisters for Life"

Once you and your students have identified instances of author's craft, we believe it is important to name the strategies and to empower students to try out the strategies in their own writing. These lesson ideas provide you with opportunities for your students to practice the strategies with support from you and their peers.

Transitional Phrases to Signal a Flashback

Teach students that a flashback should be signaled with a phrase that eases the transition to a past event.

1. Display the flashback from the excerpt "Sisters for Life." Have students locate the transitional phrases that alert the reader to the flashback.

> *My mind drifted back ten months* to the very first time I met Juliette, our foreign exchange student who had come all the way from France. *I remembered how...*

2. Brainstorm additional phrases that could be used to replace these phrases and/ or provide students with the following: *I remembered one time when..., I remembered back to the time when..., I began to think about...,* or *I started to recall...*

3. Provide students with texts that include flashbacks and ask them to highlight the transitional phrases. For example, *Dakota Dugout* by Ann Turner or *Sarah, Plain and Tall* by Patricia MacLachlan.

4. Have students add a flashback to their own writing pieces, choosing a transitional phrase from the brainstormed list or creating their own.

Flash-Forward

Teach students that a flash-forward is another strategy for weaving in key information about a character or an event. The author stops the chronological sequence of events and makes the character think about a moment or scene that might happen in the future.

1. Choose a story that students know well. Have a discussion about the main character's traits, feelings, and desires.

2. Guide students in locating a page or specific part of the book in which a flash-forward would be helpful to readers.

3. Together with students, decide the purpose for stopping the chronological action of the story and adding a flash-forward in which the main character thinks to the future. For example, students might decide to give readers a glimpse of the character in a scene in which her wishes come true or a glimpse of a scene in which the character is solving a problem.

4. Brainstorm transitional phrases that will signal to the readers that the chronological time sequence is stopping and that they are entering into a flash-forward. Bring students back to the excerpt "Sisters for Life." Point out how the author signals this meaningful scene by beginning her flash-forward with the repeated phrase: *I imagined myself.*

5. Write a flash-forward with students and reread the story, including the flash-forward. Discuss: How does the flash-forward help readers understand the character or events?

6. Have students revisit their own writing pieces and flag a place to add a flash-forward.

Extension

Invite students to explore flash-forwards by thinking of the transitions as scenes and enacting the scenes in groups.

1. Organize students into groups of three. Have them break up the flash-forward into three scenes: Present time before the flash-forward, flash-forward, and the return to the present time.

2. Have each of the three students in the group choose one of the scenes and act it out.

3. After rehearsing the scenes together and practicing a fluid transition, invite groups to present their scenes to others.

AAAWWUBBIS Words (After, Although, As, When, While, Until, Because, Before, If, Since)

Teach students the mnemonic device for recalling subordinating conjunctions (AAAWWUBBIS), and demonstrate how a comma joins the dependent clause and the main clause in order to express meaning.

1. Display the following chart (Anderson 2005), and work together with students to create sentences that fit the pattern.

Beginning Clause	Comma	Main Clause
After I ran the road race	,	I ate two bagels and a banana.
Although	,	
As	,	
When	,	
While	,	
Until	,	
Because	,	
Before	,	
If	,	
Since	,	

2. Invite students to share their observations about the beginning clauses. Discuss how the beginning clause requires the main clause to complete a thought.

3. Have students work in groups of three to hunt for the AAAWWUBBIS sentence structure in a disposable or reproducible text, such as newspaper articles, circling or highlighting them as they are found.

4. Invite students to creatively "perform" one of the found sentences for the class with one student being the beginning clause, one being the comma, and another being the main clause.

5. Send students back to their own writing pieces and have them revise two sentences for the AAAWWUBBIS sentence structure.

Dialogue and Dialogue Tags

Remind students how the author of "Sisters for Life" chooses her words for dialogue in a purposeful way. For example, instead of choosing to let us hear everyday a conversation at the breakfast table such as, "Pass the butter, please," she chooses to have the characters talk about the special times they have shared together, letting the reader in on the details of their relationship. Teach students that dialogue tags help to convey the important meaning.

1. Display the following dialogue from the excerpt: ***A little giggle slipped out*** and I said, "I won't ever forget dancing in the elevator in California." ***Juliette laughed and replied,*** "or toilet paper volleyball!"

2. Ask students what they notice about the highlighted words. Explain that the highlighted words are called dialogue tags and that dialogue tags can show readers how the characters feel as they are talking.

3. Share the following chart with students and invite them to share their observations.

Dialogue	Dialogue with Dialogue Tags
"Tomorrow is the championship hockey game," Rob said.	"Tomorrow is the championship hockey game," Rob muttered, looking down at the floor. "The season will be over," he complained. "Tomorrow is the championship hockey game," Rob boasted, pretending to hoist a trophy high above his head.

4. Together with the class, brainstorm a list of dialogue tags, using the Internet to research if possible.

5. Guide students in shared writing to create dialogue and dialogue tags for the following scenario:
Trinity and her mother discuss how tomorrow is opening day for the play at the local community theatre. Trinity has the lead.
Write dialogue to show their conversation about this.

In **shared writing**, the teacher and students come up with ideas for the story together. The teacher writes the story down as it unfolds.

6. Invite students to try the use of dialogue tags independently for the following scenario:

Susan went to a fundraiser with her mother, Barbara. Paintings were for sale, and the funds collected would go toward helping to rebuild the area after a hurricane. Susan ended up being the highest bidder for one of the paintings, and she paid for it. Write dialogue to show what Susan and Barbara said to each other after Susan found out she won the bid.

Emotional Ending

Explain that writers use the strategy of creating an emotional ending when they want to leave the reader with the same feeling that is communicated throughout the book, whether it is a feeling of sadness, joy, anger, or concern.

1. Revisit the ending of "Sisters for Life." Discuss how the author writes the following ending: *In that moment, I knew I would miss her, and I still miss her today.* Ask students to share what words from the ending strike them or tug at their heart. Discuss how the overall emotion of the story is one of sadness because it is the last breakfast the narrator and Juliette will share before saying goodbye.

2. Have students examine emotional endings in mentor texts. Gather two mentor texts: a text with a sad emotional ending and a text with a joyful emotional ending. Share the texts with students and guide them in completing the following chart to explore how the ending works.

Title of Story	Overall Emotion of the Story	Record the Ending	Does the ending leave the reader with the same overall emotion? Why?	What words or phrases in the ending strike you or tug at your heart?

Extension

- Have students think of an emotional time. In their writer's notebooks, invite them to try the strategy of writing an emotional ending. Tell students to write *just* the ending of the story they are thinking about.

- Invite students to share their ending with the class. Ask: What words or phrases strike you or tug at your heart?

- Read a story to the class stopping before the ending. Invite students to write an emotional ending of their own that would make sense to the story. Display all of the endings, including the text of the ending from the book, in a gallery walk. Encourage students to walk from piece to piece and read the endings, discussing the following:

  ☆ How do the endings make you feel? What specific words or phrases communicated that feeling?

  ☆ How are the endings alike? Different?

  ☆ Which ending is the author's ending, and what did the author do to create an emotional ending?

Reflection Questions

1. What narrative fiction writing strategies (aka, "pigeons") can you identify and name in the mentor texts you read? How about in the mentor texts your students write?

2. Which narrative fiction writing strategies are word-level strategies? Sentence-level strategies? Whole-text strategies? Why is it important to teach strategies that address all three levels?

Chapter 3

Poetry

As we guide students to discover the pigeons that are tucked up the sleeves of magician-poets, we remember the important words of poet Georgia Heard:

> When I read a poem I first let it affect my heart. My curiosity about the poem begins with amazement and love. And my eagerness to search deeper into analyzing a poem's craft comes from my yearning as a poet to know my craft better, so I can better express my heart (1999, 43).

Many of us might recall experiences with poetry that left us feeling disengaged due to inspecting poems in mechanical ways. In fact, Heard explains that traditional ways of analyzing a poem can "alienate many people from the world of poetry" (1999, 21).

How do we, as teachers, instill within our students a love for poetry *and* for the craft strategies involved in writing poetry—strategies that communicate to others what our hearts want to say? Heard suggests three layers of reading a poem.

First, she recommends introducing students to poems that are "immediately accessible, nonthreatening, and relevant to student's lives" (Heard 1999, 21). For this reason, we are using mentor texts from Amy Ludwig VanDerwater, who writes poems that speak directly to children. We find that children save her poems and cherish her poems as if they were friends. Students will greatly enjoy getting to know her work and making visible her expert use of craft strategies.

Heard also explains that we need to "help students connect personally to a poem by guiding them toward finding themselves and their lives inside a poem" (34). This resource provides lesson ideas that encourage personal connections and presents craft as the way to communicate our inner thoughts and the larger truths of life. We also believe that the process of finding ourselves in a poem begins with the opportunity to jot down our thoughts as we experience it.

Each student brings his or her own worldview and prior knowledge to construct meaning; therefore, there is no right or wrong way to make notes about a poem. We share examples of how we have jotted down our thoughts while reading the poems that follow in this chapter; however, each student will provide unique reactions, wonderings, and findings. Our models serve to show that the task of interacting with a poem on paper is quite open-ended and particular to the reader. Each student's jottings will look different; jotting notes is a personal matter and provides a special space and time for students to make meaning of their reading.

Finally, Heard suggests that we "guide students toward analyzing the craft of a poem, figuring out how a poem is built, interpreting what a poem means, or unlocking the puzzle of a difficult poem" (1999, 43). She recommends having students study the craft in small groups, each group examining the poem for a different "poetry tool," such as line-breaks or metaphor. We suggest you provide groups with an opportunity to explore each poem through the lens of a particular area; then, gather the class together for a close read to reveal the craft strategies.

Of course, each poem presents a variety of strategies. For the purposes of this text, we chose a handful of strategies to highlight in an effort to teach them well.

With Amy Ludwig VanDerwater's permission, we reveal the pigeons she uses to craft magical poems. We invite your students to get to know Amy as a mentor poet, discovering the craft strategies she chooses to use and finding patterns of style across her poems.

Writing Strategies Used in Poetry

The poems in this chapter model the artful use of specific craft strategies. Through close reading, we identify the following writing strategies, and we discuss how the writer uses strategies to communicate and enhance the meaning of the poems.

Word Choice: By choosing precise words with purpose, writers clarify meaning and provide details. Precise word choice allows readers to create mental images in their mind and can be used to show a character's motivations or feelings.

Line Breaks: Writers can emphasize, enhance, or even change meaning by playing with the lines breaks of a poem. The decision of where to end a line within a poem impacts the message they want to convey.

Alliteration: The repetition of beginning consonant sounds can be used to convey the mood of what is happening in a poem. Alliteration also creates pacing—how quickly or slowly the reader reads a section of the poem.

Circular Ending: A circular ending is when the writer begins and ends his or her writing piece by repeating a meaningful word, phrase, or idea. Circular endings can be used to highlight a character's realization or to mirror a cycle of change within the content of the poem.

Varying Length of Stanzas: Poets might follow a long stanza with a short stanza or vice versa to create mood or to emphasize a point. By juxtaposing long and short stanzas, the writer can contrast moments in a poem, highlight a change in events, or a change within a character.

Repetition: By repeating specific words or phrases, a writer can convey rhythm and movement and show the passage of time.

Syllables: Syllables can be used to establish the mood of the events or characters in a poem.

Strong Verbs: Strong verbs allow the reader to picture the specific actions of characters, objects, or forces in a poem. Strong verbs also convey exact expressions, feelings, or motivations of the characters.

Varying the Length of Sentences: Short sentences might communicate ideas such as time passing quickly. They can also be used to emphasize a message. By juxtaposing short and long sentences, writers can address feelings, events, and pacing.

Personification: By giving human qualities to nonliving things or to inanimate objects or forces, poets can paint a picture in the reader's mind, showing their behavior, attitude, actions, and intentions

Metaphor: A metaphor is a figure of speech in which the author uses one thing to represent another. The reader infers the implied relationship. The use of a metaphor activates the senses and imagination, highlighting meaning for the reader.

Point of View (first person): By speaking directly to the reader, the writer can communicate important life messages and encourage readers to connect to the text.

You will find a clean "student copy" of each mentor text in Appendix B. If you think your students will be able to understand, or at least get the gist of the text on their own, begin by providing them with copies of the text, have them read it independently (or with a partner), and annotate it as they read. In their jottings, they should note text features (e.g., italicized words, headings, and key words), interesting or unfamiliar use of language, the organizational structure of the text, questions the text raises for them, author's craft (e.g., alliteration, metaphor, varied sentence constructions, effective leads, transitions, and conclusions). If you think the text may be too challenging for your students to comprehend independently, distribute the clean copy and then engage in a guided close read. (See the next two sections for guidance.)

Once students have read and annotated the text (i.e., completed their "jottings"), call them together into a large group to discuss the content of the text (i.e., *What* does the text say?) and then to investigate how the author crafted the text (i.e., *How* does the text say it?). Rather than share our sample jottings directly with your students, we envision that you will use our annotations to help guide your students through the close readings.

Mentor Text: "Round and Round"

Round and Round

Her beak filled
with twigs
from here
        and there
she gathers
arranges them
into a nest.

Mother Bird lays
three perfect eggs
They hatch.
They grow.
They pass the test
flying away
on fuzzy wings
as Mother Bird
alone
now sings
songs of sun
in southern skies.

The nest blows down.

Mother Bird flies
farfaraway
from her home
on the ground.

Twigs become
nest becomes twigs.

Round and round.
© Amy LV

Additional Thoughts:
What do you wonder? What did you discover? What do you want to discuss?

Sample Jottings: "Round and Round"

Mentor Text: "Round and Round"

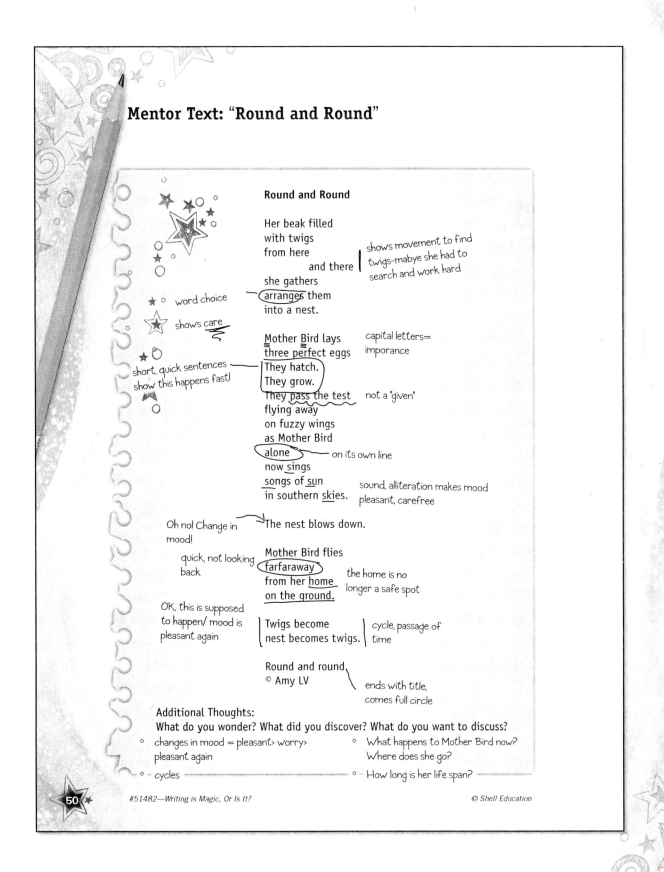

Round and Round

Her beak filled
with twigs
from here
            and there | shows movement to find
                          twigs-mabye she had to
she gathers   search and work hard
arranges them
into a nest.

word choice

shows care

Mother Bird lays   capital letters=
three perfect eggs   imporance
They hatch.
They grow.
short, quick sentences
show this happens fast!
They pass the test   not a "given"
flying away
on fuzzy wings
as Mother Bird
alone   — on its own line
now sings
songs of sun   sound, alliteration makes mood
in southern skies.   pleasant, carefree

Oh no! Change in   The nest blows down.
mood!

        quick, not looking   Mother Bird flies
        back   farfaraway   the home is no
                             from her home   longer a safe spot
                             on the ground.

OK, this is supposed
to happen/ mood is   Twigs become   cycle, passage of
pleasant again   nest becomes twigs. time

                       Round and round.
                       © Amy LV   ends with title,
                                           comes full circle

Additional Thoughts:
What do you wonder? What did you discover? What do you want to discuss?
° changes in mood = pleasant> worry>   ° What happens to Mother Bird now?
   pleasant again   Where does she go?
° cycles ——————————————— ° How long is her life span? —————

Close Reading: "Round and Round"

💬 What does the text say?

The purpose of this section is to address students' comprehension and to focus on what the text says. Here, we model how to ask text-dependent questions in order to encourage students to infer meaning.

> **Close reading** is "an instructional routine in which students critically examine a text, especially through repeated readings" (Fisher and Frey 2012, 179). Using a short passage, students read carefully to determine what the text says and to uncover specific instances of the author's craft, including items such as word choice, sentence structure, endings, leads, and more.

1. Invite student partners to share what they noticed about the poem. You might ask: What did you jot down? What strikes you? What surprises you? Guide students in figuring out what the text is saying.

2. Begin the close reading by asking: What is happening in the first stanza? Discuss the Mother Bird's motivation: What is she trying to do? What does she want? Discuss how Mother Bird is searching for twigs and how she "arranges" them. What does the word "arranges" tell us? Discuss how Mother Bird is making a home. What is the purpose of a nest?

3. Invite students to reread the second stanza. Ask: What is happening now? What is important to Mother Bird? How is Mother Bird important? Encourage student pairs to discuss: What mood is communicated in stanza two? After reading the stanza, what feeling are you left with? Students might share that the mood is carefree now that Mother Bird has completed the job she set out to do. They might respond that she is alone now, so the mood is bittersweet.

4. Direct students' attention to the next line, *The nest blows down.* Ask: What is happening? What mood is communicated now? Guide students to notice how the pace slowed as they learn that the nest blew down.

5. As you and your students read the fifth stanza, ask: Where is Mother Bird going? Why is she flying "farfaraway"? How did the story change? Why does her home no longer suit her?

6. Draw the students' attention to the lines, *Twigs become/ nest becomes twigs.* Ask: What is happening now? Discuss how the nest is being deconstructed by nature.

7. Point out how the final line, *Round and round*, matches the title. What does this phrase mean? Discuss the big ideas of cycles and change. Ask: What cycles are communicated in this poem? Discuss the life cycle of the bird as demonstrated in this poem. How do the twigs and nest show a cycle? What changes happen in Mother Bird's life? Discuss the universal truth of the passage of time. Encourage students to agree or disagree with ideas.

8. Invite students to retell the poem.

How does the text say it?

Here is the part when you invite students to reveal the pigeons tucked up the magician's sleeve. It is a good idea to share with your students what poet Georgia Heard shares with her students—that "craft cannot be separated from the meaning and feeling of a poem—that the purpose of each poetic craft is to express their feelings and experiences" (1999, 46). The intent of this section is to talk through *how* the text says what it says and to investigate the choices the author makes to reveal meaning.

1. Draw students to the title: "Round and Round." Ask: What is Amy up to? By using the precise word choice *round and round* for the title, the reader begins to think about a circular movement, right from the beginning. Discuss how the title suggests the themes of this poem: cycles in life, time passes, and change is inevitable.

2. Invite students to locate other precise word choices that communicate meaning. You might consider the following:

   - Line 6: *arranges*
     This precise word reveals the main character's motivation. Mother Bird is careful and particular in creating her home. The word *arranges* reveals that her home is meaningful to her.

   - Line 12: *test (They pass the test)*
     The word *test* is apt to evoke a sense of anxiety in readers. It is not a "given" fact that the baby birds will thrive. Knowing that the baby birds have developed and can fly on their own communicates a pleasant mood of relief and accomplishment.

   - Line 22: *farfaraway*
     The sound of this word mirrors the quick flapping of Mother Bird's wings as she flies from her home. The precise word reveals a change in motivation for Mother Bird. Her job is done; she does not look back. She has a new mission.

3. Invite students to find other precise word choices that reveal meaning.

4. This poem is also a model for artful line breaks. Ask: Where did Amy break the lines? Why?

   - Draw your students to lines three and four. Ask: Did you notice that Amy indents line number four, leaving white space before the words, *and there*? Discuss how Amy's use of line breaks shows Mother Bird's movement—how Mother Bird is searching and working hard to make a home for her family.

   - Ask: What happens to the pace of the poem when Amy uses a line break between the phrase, *Twigs become* and *nest becomes twigs*? Discuss how the arrangement shows the passing of time. It may be that Amy intended to use line breaks here to communicate the message that time passes and that there are cycles in life.

   - Encourage students to locate additional line breaks that reveal meaning. You might ask the following questions to guide students in locating artful line breaks.

- On line 16, Amy places the word *alone* on a line all by itself. What is Amy up to here? How might Mother Bird feel after her babies are off on their own? Proud? Lonely?

- Why does she write the sentence, *The nest blows down*, on a line all by itself?

- Invite students to reread the poem aloud. Ask: How do the line breaks impact the rhythm of the poem? How does Amy change this carefree mood? What does she do right after this longer, flowing stanza? Discuss the short sentence, *The nest blows down*, and how each word has just one syllable. Ask: What mood does this line communicate? Discuss words of emotion: worry, sadness, loss, and surprise. Encourage students to feel the rhythm as they read this line aloud.

5. Remind students of their previous discussion about mood. Ask: How does Amy communicate mood to us readers? What specific strategies does she use? Draw students' attention to the sound of the words in lines 17 through 18: *sings/ songs of sun/ in southern skies*. Be sure to have students read this part aloud and ask: Why does she use alliteration, or the repetition of the /s/ sound at the beginning of each word here? What meaning is she conveying to her readers?

6. Discuss how the repeated sound of /s/ communicates a soothing, peaceful, and carefree mood. Mother Bird's babies have successfully flown away and are able to take care of themselves now. Students might note that Mother Bird is relieved that the babies are healthy and flying on their own. In addition, ask students to take note of how this second stanza is structured: it is longer than the other stanzas and flows to mirror the peaceful feeling. Encourage students to feel the rhythm as they read this stanza aloud.

7. Have students share what they discover about the mood in the final three stanzas. You might point out the line breaks again in the following: *Twigs become/ nest becomes twigs*. Discuss the rhythm—how the words flow, taking the reader back to the mood of peacefulness. Discuss how this rhythm reveals the message that change is supposed to happen; change is a universal truth in life.

8. The short final line, *Round and round*, also suggests this theme in a matter-of-fact way. Change happens; that is the way it is. Point out how Amy ends her poem with the words of the title, *Round and round*. Ask: Why does she do this?

Zooming In: Analyzing Writing Strategies

Here are five strategies that the author uses that you can also implement with students using the suggested lesson ideas that follow.

1. **Precise Word Choice:** By using precise words, Mother Bird's motivation is revealed. The author uses the word *arranges* to show how Mother Bird intends to create a safe home and the word *farfaraway* to show how Mother Bird has completed her important work.

2. **Line Breaks:** Line breaks are used to emphasize, or stress, certain parts; for example, the message of change is emphasized by placing the sentence *The nest blows down* on a line of its own.

3. **Alliteration:** Alliteration, or the repetition of beginning consonant sounds, conveys a carefree, soothing mood: *sings/ songs of sun/ in southern skies*.

4. **Circular Ending:** By ending with the title, *Round and round*, Amy communicates the meaning of the big ideas: cycles and inevitable change.

5. **Varying the Length of Stanzas to Highlight a Change in Mood:** Stanza number two is the longest in the poem and communicates a peaceful, carefree mood. In contrast, the stanza that immediately follows is just one short line, contrasting the mood from carefree to loss, surprise, or sadness (students might infer different moods here).

Lesson Ideas: "Round and Round"

Once you and your students have identified instances of author's craft, we believe it is important to name the strategies and to empower students to try out the strategies in their own writing. These lesson ideas provide you with opportunities for your students to practice the strategies with support from you and their peers.

Precise Word Choice

Discuss with students how Amy's use of the precise word *arranges* reveals Mother Bird's care in creating her family's home.

1. Have students turn and talk: What image do you see in your mind when you hear the words, *she gathers/ arranges them/ into a nest*?

2. Distribute a card to each partnership that reads, *She makes them into a nest*. Discuss how the general word *makes* does not paint a clear picture in our minds.

3. Tell students that they are going to work with a partner to crack open the word *makes*. What if Amy chose to use a different word here?

4. Have partners take turns. Partner one replaces the word *makes* with a precise word, such as *drops*, *stuffs*, or *sneaks*, and partner two acts out the scene, showing the specific meaning. (You might also provide students with alternate words.)

5. As a whole class, discuss: How does the precise word reveal the character's motivations? (Is she trying to hide from predators while creating the nest? Is she sloppy and careless, hurrying to get the nest created because she is ready to lay her eggs?)

6. Have students think about another living thing that cares for his or her young. Invite students to write an original poem to reveal a character's motivation.

Line Breaks

1. Discuss how Amy uses line breaks to emphasize, or stress, certain parts. This tells readers that the meaning of this part is especially important. Borrow the fourth stanza from "Round and Round":

Mother Bird flies
farfaraway
from her home
on the ground.

2. Together with the class, read the stanza aloud, just as Amy wrote it. Record the class as you guide them in an oral reading using available audio technology, such as Audacity, VoiceThread, or iRecorder (an iPad application). Have the class listen back, reading along and paying attention to the line breaks. Ask: Where did we pick up the pace in our reading? Where did we slow down the pace? Why? What words seem to have extra-important meaning? Why?

3. Write the words on sentence strips, cutting the strips so that each word is separate.

4. Guide the class in playing with the line breaks. Read aloud the new arrangements. How do the line breaks communicate meaning? What happens if you indent the word "farfaraway?" What happens if you put the word *home* on a line of its own? What about putting the word *ground* on a line of its own?

5. Invite partners to choose a different stanza in the poem "Round and Round" and play with the line breaks.

6. Using available audio technology, invite partnerships to read each new configuration aloud and record it.

7. Discuss: How do line breaks affect meaning? How do they affect the rhythm?

8. Encourage students to choose a poem they are writing or a poem they have written in the past. Have them revise it by placing one important word on a line of its own.

Alliteration 1

1. Discuss Amy's use of alliteration and the mood it communicates to readers.

2. Visit the Library of Congress website, http://www.loc.gov/index.html, and locate a primary source photograph that communicates the mood and atmosphere of a time period your students are studying. For example, if studying flight or biographies, invite students to view a photograph depicting the Wright Brothers.

3. Have students brainstorm words that come to mind as they experience the feeling of the photograph. Accept all words, regardless of beginning sound or part of speech.

4. Once you have created a list, ask students to group words by beginning sounds. Is there a group of three or more words with the same beginning sound?

5. Invite small groups to use a thesaurus or an online source to hunt for synonyms of the remaining words. Ask: Can we find additional words that begin with the same sound and communicate the feeling of this photograph?

6. Have students write one sentence to describe the photograph using three or more words from the class list that begin with the same sound. Invite them to share.

7. Ask students to flag a spot in their current writing piece where they want to communicate mood. Have them revise using alliteration.

Extension

- Invite students to follow the alliteration with a short, direct sentence. Discuss: How does this change the feeling?

- Have students write a found poem to explore line breaks by using the site http://www.loc.gov/teachers/classroommaterials/ primarysourcesets/poetry/.

Alliteration 2

1. Have students explore different kinds of moods using music. Then, have them compare and contrast the mood created with alliteration in "Round and Round" with the moods in other alliterative texts.

2. Organize students into small groups. Have each group listen to music of a different tone (sad, upbeat, suspenseful).

3. Ask each group to write one sentence to describe the mood of the music, including at least two words that begin with the same sound.

4. Point out that writers use alliteration to create different types of moods.

5. Compare and contrast the carefree mood created with alliteration in "Round and Round" with the mood of loneliness created with alliteration in the book *The Tin*

Forest by Helen Ward (2003), which begins, "There once was a wide, windswept place…."

6. Invite students to visit The Poem Farm and locate "Poems by Technique" http://www.poemfarm.amylv.com/p/find-poem-by-technique.html.

7. Have students explore the moods that Amy creates with alliteration in her other poems.

8. Ask students to find a place in their current writing piece where they want to communicate mood. Have them revise using alliteration.

Extension

> Using the text, *All the Water in the World* by George Ella Lyon (2011), point out how the author uses alliteration to create mood, "That rain that cascaded from clouds and meandered down mountains, that wavered over waterfalls then slipped into rivers and opened into oceans…" Point out how this line is followed by a direct, short sentence: "that rain has been here before"(10).
>
> 1. Ask students to read this part aloud and to think about the mood. For example, students might respond that the mood seems peaceful and that they can sense the water flowing.
>
> 2. Point out how this line is followed by a direct, short sentence: *that rain has been here before*. Ask students to think about what happens when alliteration is followed by a short, to-the-point sentence. For example, students might respond that the short sentence highlights an important point. In this case, the author's message—that the water cycles around and moves about the earth—is highlighted in the short sentence, *that rain has been here before*.

Circular Ending

1. Read *Trout are Made of Trees* by April Pulley Sayre (2008) (or another circular text on the life cycle of a plant or animal), inviting students to discuss the circular ending, specifically the repeated words, *Trout are made of trees*.

2. Together with your class, draft a poem about the life cycle of trout, borrowing the words of Amy's circular ending, *Round and round* for your title and ending.

3. Gather a collection of life-cycle books, such as *Monarch and Milkweed* by Helen Frost (2008), *Living Sunlight: How Plants Bring the Earth to Life* by Molly Bang and Penny Chisholm (2009), and *A Grand Old Tree* by Mary Newell DePalma (2005). (Optional: Locate videos online to show the life cycle of frogs or butterflies.)

4. Invite students to choose a life cycle and draft a poem about it, borrowing the title and ending *Round and round* from Amy's poem.

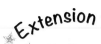 **Extension**

> Challenge students to revise their borrowed circular ending with a different word or phrase. You might brainstorm a list of words that refer to circular movement, such as *revolution*, *loop*, or *circle*. Encourage students to choose a line from their poem and use it to create the circular ending. Which circular ending is their favorite?

Varying the Length of Stanzas

1. Point out that stanza two is lengthy compared to stanza three (which is just one line). Discuss how this structure communicates a shift in mood (from carefree and peaceful to a feeling of sadness or concern) in "Round and Round."

2. Ask students to consider the question: As things change, what is left behind?

3. Have students work in groups to brainstorm things that change and the item that is left behind as a result—perhaps a molting snakes' exoskeleton or an older sibling's bedroom as she moves away. You might also encourage students to consider big ideas specific to your topic of study, such as what is left behind after a historical event or a weather event.

4. Once students have a topic and the item that is left behind, invite them to draft two stanzas.

   Stanza one: lengthy stanza describing the change

   Stanza two: one short sentence telling what is left behind

5. Discuss: What is the impact of varying your stanzas?

6. Have students revisit the poem they are working on or a poem they wrote in the past. Give them the opportunity to revise by changing the length of their stanzas.

Mentor Text: "Sea Glass"

Sea Glass

Under
Under
Under the sea
a broken bottle
waits for me.

Water washes
over glass.

Sharp turns
smooth.

Years come.
Years pass.

Someday
somewhere
on a beach
I'll spot a speck
of glass.

I'll reach
down to hold
one frosty stone
polished
by sea
for me
alone.

© Amy LV

Additional Thoughts:
What do you wonder? What did you discover? What do you want to discuss?

#51482—Writing is Magic, Or Is It?

Sample Jottings: "Sea Glass"

Mentor Text: "Sea Glass"

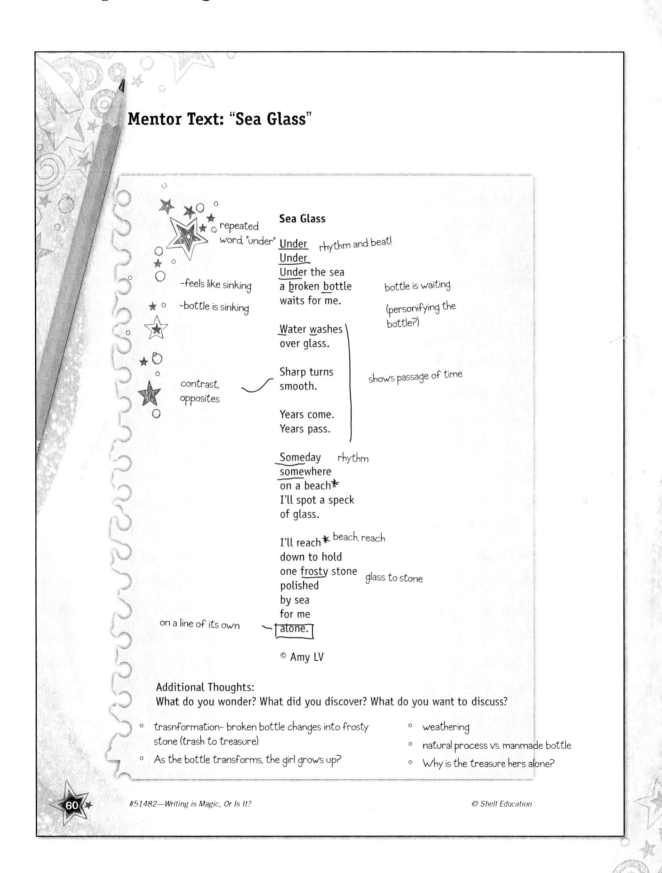

repeated word, "under"

Sea Glass

Under — rhythm and beat!
Under
Under the sea
a broken bottle   bottle is waiting
waits for me.
                          (personifying the bottle?)

-feels like sinking
-bottle is sinking

Water washes
over glass.

Sharp turns   shows passage of time
smooth.

contrast, opposites

Years come.
Years pass.

Someday   rhythm
somewhere
on a beach✱
I'll spot a speck
of glass.

I'll reach ✱ beach, reach
down to hold
one frosty stone
polished   glass to stone
by sea
for me
on a line of its own   alone.

© Amy LV

Additional Thoughts:
What do you wonder? What did you discover? What do you want to discuss?

- trasnformation- broken bottle changes into frosty stone (trash to treasure)
- As the bottle transforms, the girl grows up?
- weathering
- natural process vs. manmade bottle
- Why is the treasure hers alone?

Close Reading: "Sea Glass"

What does the text say?

The purpose of this section is to address comprehension and to focus on what the text says. Here, we model how to ask text-dependent questions in order to encourage students to infer meaning.

> **Close reading** is "an instructional routine in which students critically examine a text, especially through repeated readings" (Fisher and Frey 2012, 179). Using a short passage, students read carefully to determine what the text says and to uncover specific instances of the author's craft, including items such as word choice, sentence structure, endings, leads, and more.

1. Begin by asking students to share in small groups what they noticed about the poem. Ask: What did you jot down? What strikes you? What surprises you? Guide students in figuring out what the text is saying. Discuss: What is happening in the first stanza? What images come to mind? Discuss the feeling of sinking and how the bottle might be sinking to the ocean floor.

2. Discuss how we do not know if the main character is a boy or a girl or an adult or an animal. We do not know the narrator of this poem, but we do know that the word *me* shows first-person point of view. The person is telling the story as she sees it. Ask: What does the speaker mean when she says, *a broken bottle waits for me*? Why is the bottle waiting for her in particular? What does the character want?

3. Draw students to the second stanza. Ask: What is happening now? What is the *water*? What is the *glass*? What is the mood of this stanza? Discuss how the act of water washing over glass feels rhythmic. What is happening when *sharp turns/ smooth*? The ocean water is weathering the glass over time. What images come to mind?

4. What is revealed in the lines: *Years come./ Years pass*.? What images come to mind as you read these lines?

5. Invite students to share what is happening in the fifth stanza. What is the character's motivation? Students might share that the character is motivated to search for a treasure. The narrator is wishing. The narrator is planning. The narrator is dreaming.

6. Ask: What picture do you paint in your mind when you read the final stanza? What does *frosty stone* mean? What does the word *polished* tell us?

7. Discuss the theme of the poem: there are treasures to be found in nature for those who search and wait. Ask students what this poem reveals about weathering and processes in nature.

8. Invite students to retell the poem.

How does the text say it?

Here is the part when you invite students to reveal the pigeons tucked up the magician's sleeve. It is a good idea to share with your students what poet Georgia Heard shares with her students—that "craft cannot be separated from the meaning and feeling of a poem—that the purpose of each poetic craft is to express their feelings and experiences" (1999, 46). The intent of this section is to talk through *how* the text says what it says and to investigate the choices the author makes to reveal meaning.

1. Have students form small groups and give each group one of the following focus areas: strong verbs, repetition, rhyme, syllables, and length of sentences. Have each group discuss what they notice in regard to their area of study.

2. Bring the class together for a close read. Ask students how Amy created the feeling of sinking in the first stanza. What choices did she make to create this feeling? Students will notice the repeated word *under*. Students might notice how the repeated words *under, under, under* are stacked vertically—one word is right under the next, giving the feeling of sinking down into the sea. Discuss the choices she made with line breaks. Where did she break the lines in stanza one? Why did she make these choices?

3. Invite students to reread stanza one aloud. Ask students to notice the pace of the stanza. When we read it, do we read it slowly? Quickly? Discuss how the repetition of the word *under* creates a pattern and a beat.

4. Ask: What else does Amy do in this stanza to create a quick, rhythmic beat? Students might notice the pattern of syllables in *broken* and *bottle*. They might notice the rhyme of *sea* and *me*. Invite students to locate other examples of rhyme in the poem that help to create a rhythm and beat: *glass/ pass, beach/ reach*, and *sea/me* again in the last stanza.

5. Have students count out or clap out the rhythm of the entire poem. Ask: Does it feel as if there are any patterns? Does the beat feel regular in parts? Do the number of syllables in each line create a pattern?

6. Ask students to examine the length of her sentences. How do the length of her sentences create rhythm? Draw their attention to the following lines:
    *   Line 10: *Years come.*
    *   Line 11: *Years pass.*
    *   Discuss how these short sentences help to create a rhythm.

7. Ask students what other choices Amy made to create a rhythm. Students will likely point out repeated words in the poem (*years, some*). Why does Amy repeat these particular words? Students might point out the alliteration of *broken* and *bottle*.

8. Discuss the lighthearted mood of the poem. How does the rhythm and beat convey, or match, this mood?

9. Have students reread stanza five aloud as they clap out the syllables. Ask: Does the beat feel regular in this stanza? How does Amy create the beat in this stanza? Bring students back to the repetition of the word *some* in *someday* and *somewhere*. Ask students what Amy was up to when she repeated the /s/ sound at the beginning of *spot* and *speck*. How does the alliteration create rhythm?

10. Invite students to reread stanzas two through four. Ask students what they think Amy is up to in these three stanzas. How does Amy show us that time is passing by? Point out the feeling of motion and change. Discuss Amy's word choices of *sharp* and *smooth*. Ask: What do you notice about these words? Why does she choose words with opposite meanings? Ask students to locate additional word choices that show opposite meanings (*come* and *pass*). Discuss how Amy's word choices show the reader that the broken bottle is turning into smooth sea glass over time.

11. Together with students, reread and clap the beat of the final stanza. What do you notice about the beat? Does the rhythm within this stanza change? How? Point out the line breaks of the last three lines. Each line just has one or two words. Discuss how these line breaks slow the rhythm at the end to reveal the character's motivation: she or he intends to find the treasure. Have students find an example of a word that Amy places on a line by itself. Why does she make this decision?

12. Ask students to look carefully at Amy's choice of words in the final stanza. They are likely to notice the word *frosty*. Why does Amy use this precise word choice? What picture does it paint in your mind?

13. Bring students back to the title. Why did Amy decide to call the poem "Sea Glass" instead of "Broken Bottle" or "Pollution," for example? What meaning does she convey with the word choices *sea glass*?

Zooming In: Analyzing Writing Strategies

Here are four strategies the author used. You can also implement these with your students by following the suggested lesson ideas below.

1. **Repetition:** By repeating words, Amy gives the feeling of movement (sinking into the sea with the repetition of *under* and the movement of time with the repetition of *years* and the repetition of *some*).

2. **Syllables:** Amy uses syllables to establish a lighthearted, treasure-finding mood. Syllables also mirror the feeling of time marching on.

3. **Strong Verbs:** Strong verbs enable the reader to picture precisely what is happening.

4. **Varying the Length of Sentences:** Two-word sentences help communicate the idea that time passes quickly. The short sentences make a point.

Lesson Ideas: "Sea Glass"

Once you and your students have identified instances of author's craft, we believe it is important to name the strategies and to empower students to try out the strategies in their own writing. These lesson ideas provide you with opportunities for your students to practice the strategies with support from you and their peers.

Repetition

Repetition creates a sound and movement that can be felt with the whole body. You might notice students tapping their feet or bobbing their heads as they recite repeated words or phrases.

1. Provide students the opportunity to experience the movement of repetition with their bodies. Invite small groups to create a dance or a series of fluid movements that express the rhythm and beat of "Sea Glass." Suggest that groups repeat a movement when the text repeats a word.

2. Discuss: How does repetition create movement? How does it create the feeling of time moving/passing by?

3. Ask students to think about other things that are affected by weathering or erosion. For example, discuss what happens to the paint on buildings over time. You might also gather a collection of books, poems, videos, or podcasts that explain weathering or erosion.

4. Have students draft a poem to explore how something changes over time. Invite them to borrow the lines *Years come. Years pass.* Challenge them to add at least one additional part with repetition to communicate movement. Invite students to create dances to express the rhythm of their own poetry.

Syllables

Encourage students to internalize the rhythm of the poem "Sea Glass" and experience how the use of syllables helps to create it.

1. Provide many opportunities throughout the day to recite "Sea Glass" so that students memorize one or more stanzas in a natural way.

2. Have students use found objects around the classroom (a pencil, a shoe, or a whiteboard eraser) to tap the beat of the poem as they recite one or more stanzas. Students might also bring in found objects from home for tapping (slipper, spatula, or empty plastic bottle). Invite them to chant the poem as they tap to give the feeling of time marching on.

3. Invite students to borrow the rhythm and beat of the poem and write original lines. Challenge them to create a new beat with found objects, and write a poem to their new beat. Ask: Where do you hunt for treasures? Where do you find unexpected surprises? Yard sales? Your own backyard? In a book?

Strong Verbs

Tell students that strong verbs help us to visualize exactly what is happening in the text. Using the poem "Sea Glass," have students highlight the verbs.

1. Together with the class, compile a list of the strong verbs in "Sea Glass": *waits, washes, turns, pass, spot, reach, hold, polished.*

2. Ask students to find a spot in the classroom and take a pose, freezing like a statue.

3. Tell students that you will read the poem aloud. When they hear a strong verb, they will unfreeze and move their bodies, representing the image they see in their mind. Movements can be interpretive; they do not have to act out the word.

4. In partnerships or small groups, invite students to replace the strong verbs with other strong verbs of their choice. What happens to the picture in your mind? Encourage students to try out at least one weak verb, such as *see* for *spot*. Now, what happens to the picture in your mind? Partners take turns: reader/statue.

5. Discuss: How do strong verb choices change the picture in our minds?

6. Invite students to revisit a poem they are working on and replace at least two verbs with strong verbs.

Varying the Length of Sentences

Amy's short sentences reflect the process the glass goes through over time to make it smooth. The short sentences make the point that time causes change. With students, investigate the strategy of varying the length of sentences. Discuss the images that are evoked when they hear the short sentence *Sharp turns/ smooth*. Invite them to use short sentences to make a point by writing a poem about pollution in the ocean.

1. Have students consider the environment, specifically, pollution in the ocean. Gather a collection of texts, videos, and podcasts concerning environmental issues of the oceans, including *Tracking Trash: Flotsam, Jetsam and the Science of Ocean Motion* by Loree Griffin Burns (2010).

2. Ask: What happens to trash in the ocean? What is the impact on ocean life? What point do you want to make in your poem? What image do you want your reader to see? How can you show the passage of time using a short sentence?

3. Invite students to draft a poem. Encourage them to vary their sentences and to include at least one short sentence that shows the passage of time or what is happening to the object in the ocean.

4. For additional support, you might take a photo from *Tracking Trash*. Label the poem (which will later become the title of the poem) and consider the point you want to make. Brainstorm images, writing each image on an index card. Use the cards to draft a poem.

Mentor Text: "Asters"

Asters

Summer passed
firefly-fast.
Now dancing asters
have a blast
as golden roadsides
roll in shawls
of fuzzy faces
soft and small.

Violet
fireflake
snowworks
call –

Love now.
We will not last.
It's fall.

© Amy LV

Additional Thoughts:
What do you wonder? What did you discover? What do you want to discuss?

Sample Jottings: "Asters"

Mentor Text: "Asters"

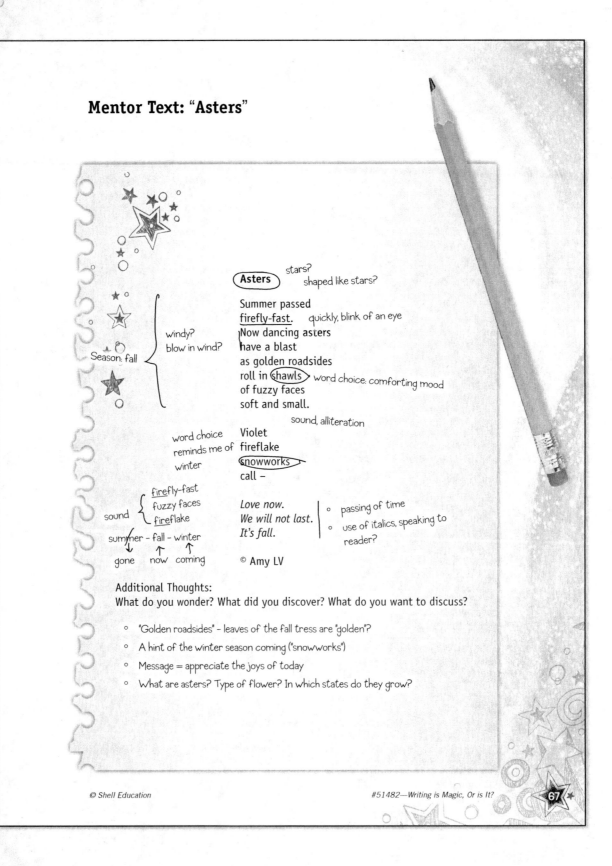

Asters — stars? shaped like stars?

windy?
blow in wind?

Season: fall

Summer passed
firefly-fast. — quickly, blink of an eye
Now dancing asters
have a blast
as golden roadsides
roll in shawls — word choice: comforting mood
of fuzzy faces
soft and small.
       sound, alliteration

word choice — Violet
reminds me of — fireflake
winter — snowworks
call –

sound — firefly-fast
       fuzzy faces
       fireflake

summer - fall - winter
  ↓   ↑   ↑
gone now coming

Love now.
We will not last.
It's fall.

© Amy LV

- passing of time
- use of italics, speaking to reader?

Additional Thoughts:
What do you wonder? What did you discover? What do you want to discuss?

- "Golden roadsides" - leaves of the fall tress are "golden"?
- A hint of the winter season coming ("snowworks")
- Message = appreciate the joys of today
- What are asters? Type of flower? In which states do they grow?

Close Reading: "Asters"

💬 What does the text say?

The purpose of this section is to address students' comprehension and to focus on what the text says. Here, we model how to ask text-dependent questions in order to encourage students to infer meaning.

Close reading is "an instructional routine in which students critically examine a text, especially through repeated readings" (Fisher and Frey 2012, 179). Using a short passage, students read carefully to determine what the text says and to uncover specific instances of the author's craft, including items such as word choice, sentence structure, endings, leads, and more.

1. Begin by asking students to share with a partner what they noticed about the poem. Ask: What did you jot down? What strikes you? What surprises you? Guide students in figuring out what the text is saying.

2. Begin the close read by discussing the title. What are *asters*? Most likely, students will not know that asters are flowers, although they might infer this from the text. Explain that asters are a type of flower and show them a photograph (perhaps from the Internet). Discuss the first two lines: *Summer passed/ fire-fly fast.*

3. What do the words *fire-fly fast* mean? What image do you picture in your mind? Discuss the nature of fireflies and how their lights blink quickly. Discuss how summertime passed quickly.

4. Ask students to describe what they picture when they hear the words, *Now dancing asters/ have a blast.*

5. What do the words *dancing* and *blast* make you feel? In what way might the asters be dancing? Discuss how the asters might be blowing in the wind. Ask about the mood of this image. Discuss the joyful tone of the image.

6. Read aloud lines five through eight, the remainder of stanza one. Draw students' attention to the lines: *as golden roadsides/ roll in shawls.* Ask: What images do you see in your mind? What makes the roadsides golden? Discuss the different images that the word *golden* is likely to evoke: the color gold and the idea of something precious and special.

7. Point out the verb *roll*. In what way do the roadsides roll? What does it mean when the roadsides roll in *shawls*? Students might not know the meaning of the word *shawls*. Show students a picture of a shawl; or, if possible, bring in a shawl so that students can touch it and experience what it feels like. Discuss how a shawl feels. Continue to read the following line, which completes the image: *of fuzzy faces/ soft and small.* What does the word *faces* mean? In what way might a flower have a face?

8. Read aloud the entire stanza again. What images come to mind? Is the road a country road? Along a highway? Ask students to describe the exact images they see in their minds.

9. Together with students, read aloud stanza two. Ask students to describe what is happening in this stanza. What does the word *snowworks* make you picture?

Discuss the thought of winter. How do the flowers appear like snow at this point in the poem? The seasons have changed from summer to fall, and this line hints that winter is on its way.

10. Read aloud the final stanza. Ask students what images come to mind. What does this stanza mean? What happens to the asters now? Discuss how the final stanza communicates the message, or universal truth of the poem: change and the passage of time. Invite students to notice the season changes and cycles. Discuss the audience for this message. Is it for those admiring these particular asters? Is it for us readers? Does the message apply to other areas of nature? Of life?

11. Invite students to retell the poem.

🗨 How does the text say it?

Here is the part when you invite students to reveal the pigeons tucked up the magician's sleeve. It is a good idea to share with your students what poet Georgia Heard shares with her students—that "craft cannot be separated from the meaning and feeling of a poem—that the purpose of each poetic craft is to express their feelings and experiences" (1999, 46). The intent of this section is to talk through *how* the text says what it says and to investigate the choices the author makes to reveal meaning.

1. Have students form small groups and give each group one of the following focus areas: personification, metaphor, alliteration, point of view, or word choice. Have each group discuss what they notice in regard to their area of study and share their thoughts with the class.

2. Bring the class together for a close read. Begin by discussing how the summer passed quickly and the surprising word choice *fire-fly-fast*. Ask students to infer what Amy is up to here. Why does she choose to use this particular word? Discuss the alliteration and how the repeated beginning /f/ sound quickens the pace of the reading, giving the feel of summer moving along quickly.

3. Ask students to reread stanza one. How does Amy make the beauty of nature come alive for us? What does she choose to do? Discuss her choice to use personification as a way to create an image in our mind. Ask students to locate examples of personification in the first stanza. Discuss how the asters dance, the roadsides roll, and the flowers have faces.

4. Ask students to locate additional examples of Amy's choice to use personification. They will likely notice that the flowers are calling and speaking the final message, *Love now./ We will not last./ It's fall.*

5. Ask students to share their most vivid image in the poem. What phrases painted a detailed image in your mind? Discuss the phrase *shawls/ of fuzzy faces/ soft and small*. Discuss what Amy was up to when she wrote this phrase. Why would Amy write that the flowers are shawls? Discuss Amy's choice to use a metaphor. When we picture a shawl in our mind, images and senses are brought forward: a sense of comfort, a soft texture, and warmth. By using metaphor, our

experiences with a shawl allow us to understand and picture the texture of the flowers.

6. Bring students' attention to the following lines: *of fuzzy faces/ soft and small.* Say the line aloud more than once. Discuss Amy's use of alliteration. Ask: Why does Amy make the choice to use alliteration in these lines? What do the repeated sounds do for the reader?

7. Discuss how there are two points of view in the poem, that of the narrator and that of the asters. By using the point of view of the asters, Amy presents an important message to her readers: stop and take in the beauty of nature while you can.

8. Draw students' attention to the word *snowworks*. Ask them what they think Amy was up to when she chose this word. Discuss the changing of the seasons and how the word *snow* makes the reader think of winter. In "Asters," summer has already passed, it is now fall, and it will soon be winter.

Zooming In: Analyzing Writing Strategies

Here are five strategies that the author uses that you can also implement with students using the suggested lesson ideas that follow.

1. **Personification:** Amy uses personification to paint a clear picture in the reader's mind, showing the true beauty of nature.

2. **Metaphor:** The use of metaphor activates the reader's sense of touch and allows the reader to imagine how the flowers feel and look.

3. **Alliteration:** Alliteration moves the pace along quickly to mirror the pace of the summer (*firefly-fast*). Amy also uses alliteration to quicken the pace and convey the feeling of rolling.

4. **Point of view:** By using the point of view of the asters in the last stanza, Amy communicates an important life message to the readers: stop and notice the beauty of nature.

5. **Word choice:** Precise word choices reveal the season and hints of the season to come (*golden, snowworks*) in addition to showing the beauty of nature.

Lesson Ideas: "Asters"

Once you and your students have identified instances of author's craft, we believe it is important to name the strategies and to empower students to try out the strategies in their own writing. These lesson ideas provide you with opportunities for your students to practice the strategies with support from you and their peers.

Personification

1. Invite students to choose one phrase from "Asters" that shows the strategy of personification.

2. Have students recreate the image they see in their mind using watercolor paint.

3. Hang the student paintings along with the words from the poem that show the personification. Invite students to take a gallery walk, noting words and phrases that come to mind on a clipboard as they view the paintings.

4. Hand out photographs of nature (perhaps images from a calendar or from the Internet).

5. Invite students to write a phrase or sentence using personification to show the beauty of nature as shown in the photograph.

6. Brainstorm with students other aspects of nature that "wow" them. Have them write lines or phrases with personification to reveal the beauty and awe.

Metaphor

Bring in a shawl and allow students to feel the texture. Discuss other metaphors that Amy might have chosen to use. What else has a soft and fuzzy texture?

1. Discuss the differences between metaphor and simile. Together with the class, turn the metaphor into a simile, such as *the asters are as fuzzy as a shawl.*

2. Have students immerse themselves in poems with metaphors by visiting the Poem Farm and reading the poems under the category: Metaphors and Similes http://www.poemfarm.amylv.com/p/find-poem-by-technique.html.

3. Ask students to record the phrases that show the strategy of metaphor and to consider how the metaphor helps the writing.

4. Bring in a collection of items from nature, and invite students to write a metaphor.

5. Have students flag one place to add a metaphor in a poem they are currently working on or a poem they have already published.

6. Discuss: Does your metaphor help your writing? Why?

#51482—Writing is Magic, Or Is It? © *Shell Education*

Extension

Invite students to visit The Poem Farm http://www.poemfarm.amylv.com/ to explore additional poems with metaphor. You will find these poems under the category "Metaphors and Similes." Have students explore the use of metaphor in poems such as "Campfire."

Alliteration

Have students visit The Poem Farm online and listen to Amy read the poem "Paper Airplane."

1. Ask students to listen for alliteration as the poem is read.

2. Invite students to discuss in small groups how alliteration enhances the meaning of the poem.

3. Encourage students to choose another object that moves and use alliteration to write a poem about it.

Point of View

Reread the ending of "Asters" and discuss how the message is from the point of view of the asters.

1. Conduct an online search for "Poems for Two Voices," and visit The Poem Farm to find examples of poems for two voices.

2. Together with students, turn "Asters" into a poem for two voices that shows the point of view of the person admiring the asters and the point of view of the asters themselves. If they were to have a conversation, what would it sound like? What would they say to one another?

3. Discuss how using point of view highlights the important message: time is passing and the beauty will not last.

4. Encourage students to choose a different aspect of nature that changes with time. For example, you might list a chrysalis, a raindrop on a petal, and an unhatched egg.

5. Invite students to draft a poem that includes the point of view of an item from nature and the message to stop and take note while we can.

Word Choice

Take advantage of a heavy rainstorm to teach precise word choice.

1. If the rainstorm happened overnight, ask: What words did you hear? What words did you see? Feel? Compile a class list, accepting all responses and parts of speech such as *bang*, *drip-drip-drip*, *sleepy*, *dark*, *pounding*, and *cold*.

2. If the storm happens during the school day, stop to record precise words that come to mind.

3. Allow students to hear a podcast or video of a different type of weather event that *wows* them. Have them brainstorm precise words as they listen.

4. Invite students to circle at least two general words in a poem they are working on. Challenge them to replace the words with precise words.

Extension

Invite students to take notice of the clever way that Amy invents her own words to communicate images, and how she does this across her work (*farfaraway*, *firefly-fast*, and *snowworks*).

When discussing her poem "*Asters*," Amy wrote on her blog: "Was I inspired by a favorite poem here? I am certain that I was. X. J. Kennedy's poem "Blow-Up" speaks of a cherry tree losing its blossoms. It, too, rhymes the words *blast* and *last*. It, too, is about time's fast passage."

1. Have students compare and contrast the poems, paying attention to the images they see in their minds and the strategies used.

2. Invite students to create a visual to depict the similarities and differences of the poems.

Reflection Questions

1. How does using specific strategies help to communicate meaning?

2. What strategies do you find most helpful to you as a writer? Why?

Chapter 4

Informative/Explanatory Writing

A recent survey conducted by the National Endowment for the Arts (2012) found, "More than half of American adults read a work of literature or a book (fiction or nonfiction) not required for work or school. However, adults' rates of literary reading (novels or short stories, poetry, and plays) dropped back to 2002 levels (from 50 percent in 2008 to 47 percent in 2012)" (as cited in Waldman 2013, para. 1). Using this finding, Katy Waldman (2013) suggested, "Since general reading rates have remained constant, that must mean we are reading a lot more nonfiction" (para. 3). We are not surprised by these findings and have witnessed a surge in nonfiction reading and writing in K–12 schools. Perhaps this is the case in your school, too. You are likely to have your students respond to reading by annotating texts while reading; recording how they work through a math problem; taking notes, writing drafts, or creating storyboards while preparing research reports; listing procedures they use in science experiments; and publishing feature articles in a school newspaper.

National standards expect students to read texts that are 50 percent literary and 50 percent informational in grade four; 45 percent literary and 55 percent informational in grade 8; and 30 percent literary and 70 percent informational across the disciplines in grades 6–12 (http://www.corestandards.org/ELA-Literacy/introduction/key-design-consideration). Informational/explanatory writing, as defined by the Common Core State Standards (CCSS), is writing that "conveys information accurately" (Appendix A, 23) and includes such genres as "literary analyses, scientific and historical reports, summaries, and précis writing as well as forms of workplace and functional writing, such as instructions, manuals, memos, reports, applications, and résumés" (Appendix A, 23).

Let us begin our exploration of this genre by looking at the skills and understandings identified in the English Language Arts Standards for Writing Informative/Explanatory Texts (CCSS 2010 available at http://www.corestandards.org/ELA-Literacy/W/introduction). These standards reflect what students should know and be able to do by the end of the identified academic year. As you look horizontally across the rows in Figure 4.1, you will find the skills and understandings associated with writing informational texts in grades 3–8. Looking vertically down each column, you will see how each skill or understanding increases in complexity. Rather than rewrite the Common Core State Standard in each box, we included only changes/additions from grade to grade, as reflected in the language taken directly from the standards.

A **précis** is a concise, academic summary or abstract.

Figure 4.1: Common Core State Standards Expectations for Writing Informative/Explanatory Texts

Grade	Skills and Understandings Students Must Demonstrate by the End of Each Grade					
	Introduce a Topic	Develop a Topic	Link ideas/ Transitions	Precise Language	Formal Style	Concluding Statement
Grade 3	Introduce a topic and group related information together; include illustrations when useful to aiding comprehension.	Develop the topic with facts, definitions, and details.	Use linking words and phrases (e.g., also, another, and, more, but) to connect ideas within categories of information.	N/A	N/A	Provide a concluding statement or section.
Grade 4	Group information in paragraphs and sections; include formatting, illustrations, and multimedia when useful to aiding comprehension.	… concrete details, quotations, or other information and examples related to the topic.	Link ideas within categories of information using words and phrases (e.g, another, for example, also, because).	Use precise language and domain-specific vocabulary to inform about or explain the topic.	N/A	… related to the information or explanation presented.
Grade 5	Introduce a topic clearly; provide a general observation and focus, and group related information logically…	Same as Grade 4	Link ideas within and across categories of information using words, phrases, and clauses (e.g., in contrast, especially)	Same as Grade 4	N/A	Same as Grade 4

Grade	Skills and Understandings Students Must Demonstrate by the End of Each Grade					
	Introduce a Topic	Develop a Topic	Link ideas/ Transitions	Precise Language	Formal Style	Concluding Statement
Grade 6	... Organize ideas, concepts, and information using strategies such as definition, classification, comparison/ contrast, and cause/effect...	Develop the topic with relevant facts...	Use appropriate transitions to clarify the relationships among ideas and concepts.	Same as Grade 4	Establish and maintain a formal style.	... follow from the information or explanation presented.
Grade 7	Introduce a topic clearly, previewing what is to follow...	Same as Grade 6	Use appropriate transitions to create cohesion and clarify...	Same as Grade 4	Same as Grade 6	... follow from and support the information or explanation presented.
Grade 8	...Organize ideas, concepts, and information into broader categories...	Develop the topic with relevant, well-chosen facts...	Use appropriate and varied transitions to create...	Same as Grade 4	Same as Grade 6	Same as Grade 7

The CCSS guide our thinking, and the following texts from the Library of Congress serve as appropriate mentor texts for elementary- and middle-school writers: "The 4th of July in Colorado," "The Corn Palace," "Louis' Lunch," and "Bean-Hole Beans."

Writing Strategies Used in Informative/Explanatory Writing

The information/explanatory pieces in this chapter model the use of specific craft strategies. Through close reading, we identify the following writing strategies, and we discuss how the writer uses strategies to communicate and to enhance the meaning of the writing.

You will find a clean "student copy" of each mentor text in Appendix B. If you think your students will be able to understand, or at least get the gist of the text on their own, begin by providing them with copies of the text, have them read it independently (or with a partner), and annotate it as they read. In their jottings, they should note text features (e.g., italicized words, headings, and key words), interesting or unfamiliar use of language, the organizational structure of the text, questions the text raises for them, author's craft (e.g., alliteration, metaphor, varied sentence constructions, effective leads, transitions, and conclusions). If you think the text may be too challenging for your students to comprehend independently, distribute the clean copy and then engage in a guided close read. (See the next two sections for guidance.)

Once students have read and annotated the text (i.e., completed their "jottings"), call them together into a large group to discuss the content of the text (i.e., *What* does the text say?) and then to investigate how the author crafted the text (i.e., *How* does the text say it?). Rather than share our sample jottings directly with your students, we envision that you will use our annotations to help guide your students through the close readings.

"I Think": Students use this lead strategy to create a comprehensive opening sentence that reveals the topic of the text and what the author thinks about this topic.

Show, Don't Tell: As the name suggests, this strategy allows writers to show rather than explicitly state the information they share.

Commas with Non-Essential Information: This strategy explores how and why writers weave in phrases that contain interesting, but not critical, information.

Commanding Leads: This common lead strategy hooks readers by drawing them directly into the text. Words such as "Imagine" or "Look at" are often used.

Begin with a Verb: As a way to add variety to sentence beginnings, this strategy invites students to play with verbs as sentence openers.

Building Bridges Between Ideas: This transition strategy enables writers to create cohesion between and among sentences by paying attention to how the sentences work together.

Why/How?: This common nonfiction organizational strategy focuses on why a new idea or invention is useful or necessary and how it is realized.

Adding Details with Adverbs: This strategy focuses on using adverbs to tell why, how, when, and under what condition something is happening or has happened.

Why a Colon?: Colons often signal a list, which is the grammar generalization introduced in this strategy.

Concluding with a Claim: A claim is what someone believes to be true. "Concluding with a Claim" enables writers to bring closure to an informative text by stating one (indisputable) truth about the topic.

Imperatives: This strategy offers writers opportunities to add specificity to their texts by calling attention to imperatives (command words) used in procedural writing (e.g., *stir, rake,* and *gather*).

"How-to" Organization: "How-to" texts generally follow a recognizable organizational formula, which is introduced through this strategy.

Ta-da!: Often, the conclusion of a procedural piece of writing contains a statement that applauds the reader for successfully completing the directions. The "Ta-da!" strategy encourages writers to show excitement and conclude with a bit of fanfare.

Mentor Text: "The 4th of July in Colorado"

The 4th of July in Colorado
A Local Legacy
(from Library of Congress)

Many American cities have rodeos but Greeley, Colorado, has the "Worlds' Largest Fourth of July Rodeo." The city was named after Horace Greeley, a well-known newspaperman for the New York Tribune. One of his famous sayings was "Go west, Young Man, go west. In 1869, he sent one of his reporters west to Colorado to write a story about farming. The reporter, Nathan C. Meeker, liked the area so much he stayed and started a town named after his boss. It was Meeker's vision that helped establish a successful community based on, among other qualities, cooperation, agriculture, irrigation, and education.

Every year the people of Greeley celebrate Independence Day with a rodeo. In the early days, the rodeo was a small local event, but it grew more and more popular. In 1922, more than 10,000 people came to the rodeo, and the town officially named the event the "Greeley Fourth of July Celebration and the Spud Rodeo and Horseshow." They called it the spud rodeo because spuds (another name for potatoes) are an important crop grown around Greeley. A few years later, even more people came to the rodeo, when famous cowboys started competing with the local ranch hands. Today, the rodeo lasts for two weeks and is called the Greeley Independence Stampede.

Additional Thoughts:
What do you wonder? What did you discover? What do you want to discuss?

Sample Jottings: "The 4th of July in Colorado"

Mentor Text: "The 4th of July in Colorado"

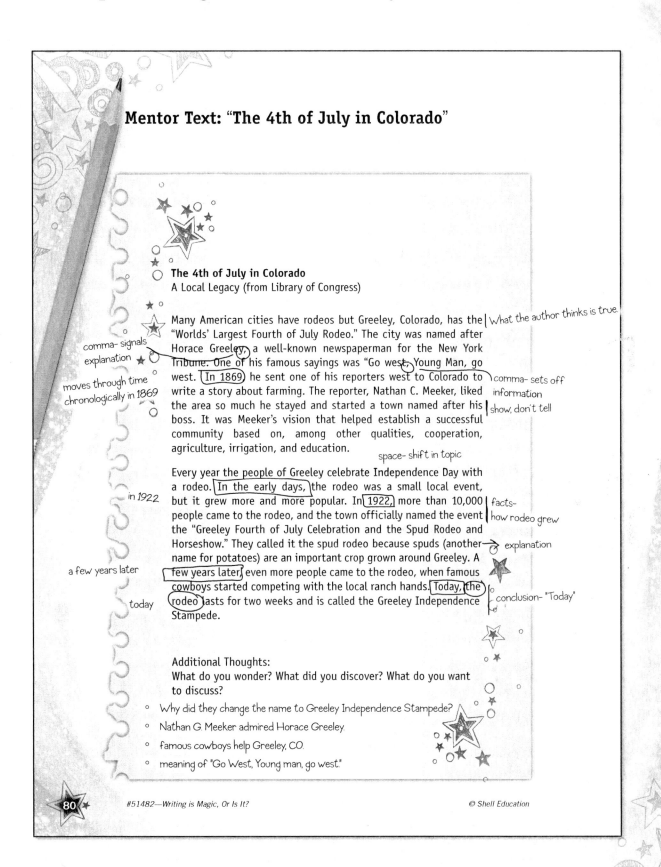

The 4th of July in Colorado
A Local Legacy (from Library of Congress)

What the author thinks is true.

Many American cities have rodeos but Greeley, Colorado, has the "Worlds' Largest Fourth of July Rodeo." The city was named after Horace Greeley, a well-known newspaperman for the New York Tribune. One of his famous sayings was "Go west, Young Man, go west. In 1869 he sent one of his reporters west to Colorado to write a story about farming. The reporter, Nathan C. Meeker, liked the area so much he stayed and started a town named after his boss. It was Meeker's vision that helped establish a successful community based on, among other qualities, cooperation, agriculture, irrigation, and education.

comma- signals explanation
moves through time chronologically in 1869

comma- sets off information
show, don't tell

space- shift in topic

Every year the people of Greeley celebrate Independence Day with a rodeo. In the early days, the rodeo was a small local event, but it grew more and more popular. In 1922, more than 10,000 people came to the rodeo, and the town officially named the event the "Greeley Fourth of July Celebration and the Spud Rodeo and Horseshow." They called it the spud rodeo because spuds (another name for potatoes) are an important crop grown around Greeley. A few years later, even more people came to the rodeo, when famous cowboys started competing with the local ranch hands. Today, the rodeo lasts for two weeks and is called the Greeley Independence Stampede.

in 1922
facts- how rodeo grew
explanation
a few years later
today
conclusion- "Today"

Additional Thoughts:
What do you wonder? What did you discover? What do you want to discuss?
- Why did they change the name to Greeley Independence Stampede?
- Nathan G. Meeker admired Horace Greeley.
- famous cowboys help Greeley, CO.
- meaning of "Go West, Young man, go west."

Close Reading: "The 4th of July in Colorado"

💬 What does the text say?

The purpose of this section is to address students' comprehension and to focus on what the text says. Here, we model how to ask text-dependent questions in order to allow students to infer meaning.

> **Close reading** is "an instructional routine in which students critically examine a text, especially through repeated readings" (Fisher and Frey 2012, 179). Using a short passage, students read carefully to determine what the text says and to uncover specific instances of the author's craft, including items such as word choice, sentence structure, endings, leads, and more.

1. After students have had time to read and annotate the article, ask them to share what they noticed about it. Students may mention the purpose of this article: to explain how Greeley, CO, was established and how its annual rodeo became so popular. You might orient them to the text by asking them to reread the first paragraph.

   - Ask: Why is the *New York Tribune* italicized? How do you know it is a newspaper? Ask: Who was Mr. Greeley? Be sure students understand why Mr. Meeker went to Colorado and then discuss what his actions showed about the type of person he was. Talk about what may have prompted him to name the community after Mr. Greeley and what Mr. Meeker valued.

2. Invite students to reread the second paragraph and discuss the shift in topics (from establishing Greeley to the rodeo). Ask students if they think the first paragraph was necessary. What purpose did it serve? Why did the author include it?

3. What word in the second paragraph lets the reader know that only people living in or close to Greeley attended the rodeo when Greeley was first established? (Answer: *local*) Linger over the words "small local event" and discuss the contrast between the early days of the rodeo and the "world's largest rodeo" of today.

4. Discuss what the famous cowboys did to make Greeley's rodeo so popular.

5. Draw students' attention back to the first sentence in the article and then to the last two sentences. Invite students to talk about why the author may have begun and concluded the article with these three sentences.

💬 How does the text say it?

In this section, we point out some of the strategies the author of "The 4th of July in Colorado" used to craft this text. In the lessons that follow, you and your students will learn more about the strategies and how to integrate them into your own writing.

1. In preparation for the whole-class discussion that follows, ask students to reread the text while paying particular attention to the introduction, places in which the author used details to reveal information, and the author's use of commas. After students have had a few minutes to read and think about the author's craft, have them talk with their partners about what they noticed in

#51482—Writing is Magic, Or Is It?

the text, and then reconvene the large group to share their thoughts. This part of the lesson should move along quickly.

2. Students may have noticed that the author does not waste any time presenting his or her belief about the 4th of July celebration in Greeley. If students do not mention the lead when they report their findings, ask: How does this lead sentence connect to the rest of the text? Why do you think the author decided to begin with what she/he believes about this topic? They may respond by saying something like, "The lead sentence is the topic sentence that captures the gist of this text. I think the author began with what she or he believes about the topic to show pride and to show why Greeley's rodeo is so special."

3. Next, guide students to see that the author used the "show, don't tell" technique when introducing Mr. Greeley. Ask: How did Greeley, CO, get its name? Discuss how honored Mr. Greeley must have felt when he heard the news. Ask: Why do you think Mr. Meeker named the town after his boss? The author does not come right out and tell us this but clearly shows it through Mr. Meeker's actions.

4. After concluding the "show, don't tell" discussion, invite students to read the following sentence to themselves: "The city was named after Horace Greeley, a well-known newspaperman from the New York Tribune." Circle the comma and point out that there are two parts in this sentence. Invite a discussion about the role of the comma (i.e., to separate essential from non-essential information).

5. Challenge students to find a spot in the article where the author used punctuation other than a comma to set off non-essential information. (Answer: *They called it the spud rodeo because spuds [another name for potatoes] are an important crop crown around Greeley.*) Have a student explain why commas could be used in this sentence and why the author may have opted for parentheses instead of commas. Although commas and parentheses serve the same purpose in setting off non-essential information from essential information in a sentence, the Purdue Online Writing Lab (OWL) makes the following distinction: "Parentheses are used to emphasize content. They place more emphasis on the enclosed content than commas" (https://owl.english.purdue.edu/owl/resource/566/01/, under Parenthesis). During this close read, students should form a tentative explanation of this grammar "rule." Formal instruction of the generalization will follow in the next section of this chapter.

Zooming In: Analyzing Writing Strategies

Here are three strategies the author used. You can also implement these with your students by following the suggested lesson ideas below.

1. **"I Think"**: This is a difficult strategy to teach and to learn because the writer must be able to usher in (make known) the **topic**, identify the **overall (main) point** he or she wants to make about the topic, and examine the writing to make sure **most of it is about this point**. As they write, writers need to ask,

"What am I *really* writing about, and what do I think about this topic?" If the report or essay is about one small, focused topic, it is often easier to create a lead than it is when the topic is broad or the text is a list of underdeveloped topics. The author of "The 4th of July in Colorado" created a lead sentence in which he or she identified a topic (4th of July), indicated the main point of the essay (Greeley, Colorado has the "world's largest Fourth of July rodeo"), and used evidence throughout the essay to support this point.

2. **Show, Don't Tell:** As the name suggests, this strategy allows writers to show rather than explicitly state the information they share. The following reveals how much Nathan Meeker admired Mr. Greeley: "The reporter, Nathan C. Meeker, liked the area so much he stayed and started a town named after his boss."

3. **Commas with Non-Essential Information:** This strategy explores how and why writers weave in phrases that contain interesting, but not critical, information as in the following sentence from the mentor text: "The city was named after Horace Greeley, a well-known newspaperman for the *New York Tribune*." The author used a comma to separate the essential part of the sentence from "extra" information.

Lesson Ideas: "The 4th of July in Colorado"

As noted in other places in this book, the writer writes so his or her intended message is as clear as possible for the reader, and the reader reads carefully in order to construct the author's intended message. Writers use strategies to help the reader understand their messages. Although we could focus on several aspects of the author's craft, we concentrate on the introduction; show, don't tell; and commas that signal non-essential information.

"I Think"

1. Use the following example, or one of your choosing, to model this strategy. Say, "Suppose I'm writing a report about chimpanzees. I briefly explain where they live and what their habitat is like. Most of my paper is about how adult chimpanzees teach young chimps to make tools that they use for different purposes. I describe, for instance, how they strip leaves off small twigs and use the twigs to 'fish' for termites, which they eat. I also describe how chimps use rocks the way people use hammers and how they use leaves as sponges."

2. "I want to write a lead sentence that will concisely capture the message I want to convey. I begin by saying to myself, "I think...," and finish the statement with the one big idea I want my readers to walk away knowing. I'm trying to decide if one of the following three leads might be effective. (1) Chimpanzees are fun; (2) Chimpanzees fish for termites; or (3) Chimpanzees make and use tools for many purposes."

3. Using a chart, such as the one that follows, model how you test your three lead sentences against the criteria we established:

	Identifies who or what the text is about	States the overall (main) point	Is mostly about this point	Comment
Chimpanzees are fun.	✔	X	X	does not express main point
Chimpanzees fish for termites.	✔	X	X	too narrow
Chimpanzees make and use tools for many purposes.	✔	✔	✔	captures main message

4. Have a second mentor text available, perhaps "Author Response: Roald Dahl" (CCSS Appendix C, 29). Read the essay with your students and ask if the lead is an effective "I Think" lead. If using the Roald Dahl text, you will see that the writer used the following lead: "Roald Dahl is a very interesting author to me." Discuss whether it meets the criteria: tells who or what the paper is about, presents an overall (main) point, and addresses the main point. The writer stated who or what the paper is about (Roald Dahl), identified the main point (that Roald Dahl is a very interesting author), and supported his point with evidence throughout, noting, for instance, that Dahl "makes up interesting words" and "uses lots of similes" (29). Emphasize that authors do not write the words "I think," but rather use these two words to help them mull over strong lead sentences.

⭐ Extension

Have students use the "I Think" strategy to revise a piece of their nonfiction or a published text, such as *Mount Rushmore National Memorial*. (http://www.americaslibrary.gov/es/sd/es_sd_mount_1.html)

Have students craft one (or more) lead sentences using the "I Think" strategy. When students are ready, have them share their leads with the large group.

Show, Don't Tell

1. Begin by sharing a piece of art and explaining that artists use details to show what they want to convey. Use the following piece of art, or one you select, and help students discover what the details reveal (show).

- Norman Rockwell's *The Runaway* http://collections.nrm.org/search.do?id=3068 13&db=object&page=1&view=detail

Where are the people in the painting? How did Norman Rockwell show this?

Do you think this is a painting of a boy who ran away from home today? How do you know? How did Norman Rockwell provide this information?

2. Discuss the importance of showing, rather than telling, and then draw students' attention to the following sentence from the article: "The reporter, Nathan C. Meeker, liked the area so much he stayed and started a town named after his boss." Ask: Why did Mr. Meeker name the town after his boss? What does this reveal/show about Mr. Meeker? Why did the author not simply say, "Mr. Meeker admired Mr. Greeley?" *Showing* makes texts more interesting to read (than if everything is explicitly stated) and allows the reader to feel connected to the author and the text.

3. Finally, display the following sentence: *It was windy*. Invite students to use details, actions, or dialogue to show, rather than tell, that it was windy (e.g., The flag pole rocked from side to side, and the flag stretched straight out).

Extension

> After students have practiced this strategy with you, invite them to revisit one of their nonfiction pieces of writing and revise it to include at least one "show, don't tell" statement.

Commas with Non-Essential Information

1. Direct students' attention back to the following sentence from the article: "The city was named after Horace Greeley, a well-known newspaperman for the *New York Tribune*." Explain that writers sometimes include information in sentences that can be interesting but not necessary for understanding or for the writer to make his or her point.

2. Try this: Set up the following sentence, similar to a poem for two voices, so Group A reads "Dalmatians," followed by Group B reading "white dogs with black spots," and then back to Group A to finish with "were once trained to lead horse-drawn fire carriages to fires." Students will hear the entire sentence. Next, have Group A read just its two parts aloud, "Dalmatians were once trained to lead horse-drawn fire carriages to fires."

3. Point out that Group A reads the essential parts of the sentence aloud, while Group B reads the non-essential part. Show how the complete sentence is written, pointing out that the commas can signal the beginning and end of non-essential parts of sentences.

Group A	Group B
Dalmatians	
	white dogs with black spots
were once trained to lead horse-drawn fire carriages to fires.	

4. Display a few more examples in which the comma serves this purpose and have students confirm (or refute) their original understanding.

It's challenging for scientists to study giant squid, the largest invertebrate on Earth, because giant squid live so deep within the ocean.

According to the Environmental Protection Agency (EPA), a government organization created to protect humans and the environment, almost 25 percent of the food people prepare each year is wasted.

- If students need more guided practice, repeat the activity using additional sentences, such as (1) *Jupiter, which is the fifth planet from the sun, has 50 known moons.* (2) *Polar bears hunt seals in the Arctic, where it's dark all winter.*

Extension

- Invite students to apply this strategy in one of their texts or another text you supply.

- Challenge students to collect examples of this strategy from the nonfiction texts they are reading.

Mentor Text: "The Corn Palace"

The Corn Palace

A Local Legacy
(from Library of Congress)

Imagine a building covered with colorful murals.
Now imagine that same building with an exterior
made entirely out of corn and other grains! This
building exists—it is the Corn Palace.
Built in 1892 in Mitchell, South Dakota, the
Corn Palace was created to dramatically
display the products of the harvest of South
Dakota's farmers, in murals on the outside of
the building. The murals are made from
thousands of bushels of corn and other
grains and grasses such as wild oats, rye,
straw, and wheat. Each year these corn
decorations are completely stripped down
and entirely new murals are created. The
Corn Palace is a great tourist attraction and
a meeting place for the community. Many
events are held here and the most popular is
the Corn Palace Stampede Rodeo. But the
horses must be watched carefully so they
don't eat the building!

Additional Thoughts:
What do you wonder? What did you discover? What do you
want to discuss?

Sample Jottings: "The Corn Palace"

Mentor Text: "The Corn Palace"

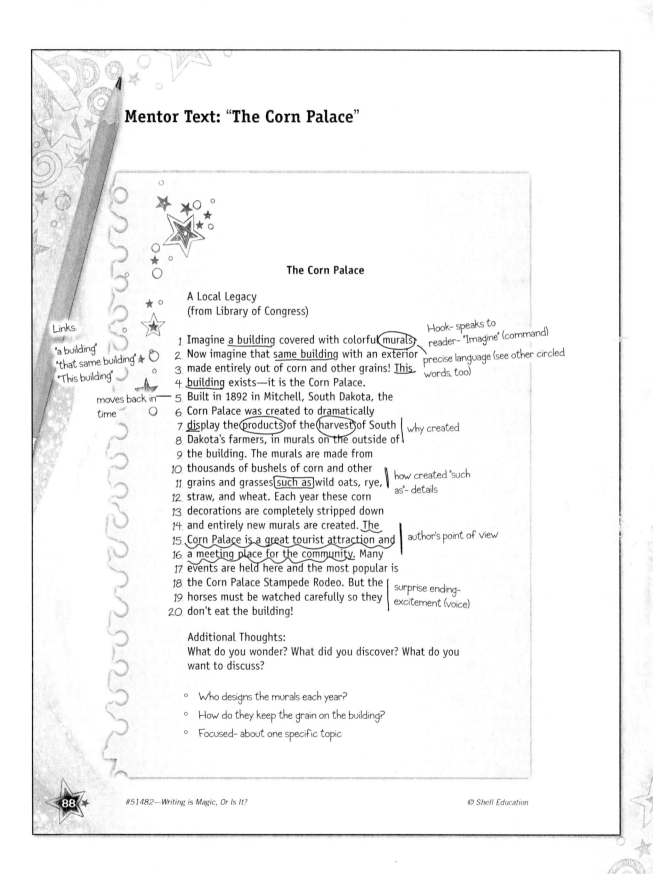

The Corn Palace

A Local Legacy
(from Library of Congress)

1. Imagine a building covered with colorful (murals)
2. Now imagine that same building with an exterior
3. made entirely out of corn and other grains! This
4. building exists—it is the Corn Palace.
5. Built in 1892 in Mitchell, South Dakota, the
6. Corn Palace was created to dramatically
7. display the (products) of the (harvest) of South
8. Dakota's farmers, in murals on the outside of
9. the building. The murals are made from
10. thousands of bushels of corn and other
11. grains and grasses [such as] wild oats, rye,
12. straw, and wheat. Each year these corn
13. decorations are completely stripped down
14. and entirely new murals are created. The
15. Corn Palace is a great tourist attraction and
16. a meeting place for the community. Many
17. events are held here and the most popular is
18. the Corn Palace Stampede Rodeo. But the
19. horses must be watched carefully so they
20. don't eat the building!

Hook- speaks to reader- "Imagine" (command)
precise language (see other circled words, too)

why created

how created "such as"- details

author's point of view

surprise ending- excitement (voice)

Links:
"a building"
"that same building"
"This building"

moves back in time

Additional Thoughts:
What do you wonder? What did you discover? What do you want to discuss?

○ Who designs the murals each year?
○ How do they keep the grain on the building?
○ Focused- about one specific topic

Close Reading: "The Corn Palace"

💬 What does the text say?

The purpose of this section is to address students' comprehension and to focus on what the text says. Here, we model how to ask text-dependent questions in order to encourage students to infer meaning.

1. Begin by asking students to talk with a partner about the meaning of the word *mural*. What is a mural? Ask: What word might you use to describe the Corn Palace mural: plain, old, or unique? Invite students to turn and talk about their answers and the evidence they used to determine the answer. You may want to follow up by asking: How do you know the murals are not plain? Are not old? What does the text tell you?

2. Pose the following questions: What did you learn about the Corn Palace? Did anything about this building surprise you?

3. Digging deeper, ask: Why do you think the author began this text the way he or she did? They may respond that the author tried to hook readers by having them use their imagination.

4. Looking at the second paragraph, ask students to explain how that paragraph built on the first paragraph. Encourage students to articulate what the author wanted readers to learn in the second paragraph and supply evidence to support their thinking. Students may say something like, "In the first paragraph, the author lets readers know that the Corn Palace is a building with a mural made of corn and other grains that cover the outside of it. In the second paragraph, the author provides the specifics (such as when it was built and what grain are used)."

5. While closely reading the second paragraph, focus on grain-specific words that convey important concepts. Ask, for instance, what the author meant by *the products of the harvest* and what words let readers know that the people who built the Corn Palace wanted everyone to notice it. The author says, for instance, "the Corn Palace was created to dramatically display the products...."

6. If students have not already done so, acknowledge that the second paragraph serves two purposes: to explain why the Corn Palace was built and how it was built. See if students can identify the sentences that provide this information.

7. Finally, call attention to the conclusion. Ask: Why do you think the author ended the article in this way? They may respond that the author ended with a humorous sentence to bring closure.

How does the text say it?

In this section, we point out some of the strategies the author of "The Corn Palace" used to craft this text. In the lessons that follow, you and your students will learn more about the strategies and how to integrate them into your own writing.

> **Close reading** is "an instructional routine in which students critically examine a text, especially through repeated readings" (Fisher and Frey 2012, 179). Using a short passage, students read carefully to determine what the text says and to uncover specific instances of the author's craft, including items such as word choice, sentence structure, endings, leads, and more.

1. Begin by helping students unpack the writer's craft as you explain how the magician created the magic. Separate students into four "focus" groups and have each group investigate one of the following topics: how the lead paragraph was written, how the first sentence in the second paragraph was constructed, how the author "bridged" one idea to the next (transitions), and how the text was organized. Invite students to share their observations with the large group and then initiate a close read, using following ideas, to expand upon your students' observations.

2. Students in the "leads" focus group will probably mention the use of the word *imagine* and then *now imagine*. Discuss how this lead pulls the reader into the text and why the author may have included both *imagine* and *now imagine*. The first paragraph, as previously noted, introduces the idea of a grain-covered mural that covers the Corn Palace. The author uses *Imagine* and *Now imagine* to hook the reader.

3. While analyzing the first paragraph, have students read to find another repeated word. They will notice that *building* appears in all three sentences, modified by a different adjective each time (*a, that same, this*). Ask students why the author repeated *building* so often and how the different adjectives provide a slightly different emphasis in each sentence.

4. Moving to the second paragraph, reread it with students, and ask them to recall how the author organized the information in it (why/how). Continue by exploring the specific details the author used to describe the murals and talk about why the author included the words *such as*. The text begins by awakening the reader's imagination, moves to the present ("This building exists..."), and then moves back in time (1892). Most of the second paragraph describes the present day Corn Palace. Students may notice other organizational structures for this text: Some students may see that this text has an introduction, a section that explains *why* and *how*, and conclusion (see previous annotation).

5. As you reread the concluding sentence, discuss the obvious change in tone. Most of the article is informative and based on facts, but the writer connects to readers in a different way in the last sentence. The author has become more playful rather than factual. Talk about how the author accomplished this change in tone and whether or not the playful tone provided an effective conclusion.

Zooming In: Analyzing Writing Strategies

Here are four strategies the author used. You can also implement these with your students by following the suggested lesson ideas below.

1. **Commanding Leads:** This common lead strategy hooks readers by drawing them directly into the text. In literature you read with your students, you may see words such as *suppose* or *look at* being used. The author of "The Corn Palace" engaged readers by using the word *imagine* in the first sentence and using *now imagine* to further connect with readers in the second sentence.

2. **Begin with a Verb:** As a way to add variety to sentence beginnings, this strategy invites students to play with verbs as sentence openers.

3. **Building Bridges between Ideas:** This transition strategy enables writers to create cohesion between and among sentences by paying attention to how the sentences work together. The author of "The Corn Palace" cleverly repeated the word *building* three times to create links, while using a different adjective each time to add specificity and interest. In lines 1, 2, and 3, the author used *a building*, *that same building*, and *this building* to move the reader through the text.

4. **Why/How?:** This common nonfiction organizational strategy focuses on why a new idea or invention was useful or necessary and how it was realized. Readers learn that the Corn Palace was built to "display the products of the harvest of South Dakota's farmers" (why) and that "the murals are made from thousands of bushels of corn and other grains and grasses such as wild oats, rye, straw, and wheat" (how).

Lesson Ideas: "The Corn Palace"

Once you and your students have identified instances of author's craft, we believe it is important to name the strategies and to empower students to try out the strategies in their own writing. These lesson ideas provide you with opportunities for your students to practice the strategies with support from you and their peers.

Commanding Lead

1. You may be familiar with Sandra Markle's *Outside and Inside* series (e.g., *Outside and Inside the Giant Squid* or *Outside and Inside Rats and Mice*). Markle calls readers into several of her books by issuing commands along the way: *plunge into* and *look at*. This same strategy can be used in lead sentences.

   - Point out how the author of "The Corn Palace" used the word *Imagine* and then *Now imagine* to invite the reader into the text. Read the following texts and discuss how the author uses *suppose* and *imagine* as the first word in the lead sentences, respectively.

   - Mark, Jan 2007. *The Museum Book* (CCSS Appendix B, 59)

   - Hall, Leslie. 2009. "Seeing Eye to Eye" (CCSS Appendix B, 75).

Ask how the commands help the writer connect to the reader.

2. Ask students to take one of their writing samples, or provide a common text, and have them revise the lead sentence using one of the following verbs: *imagine, suppose, pretend, visualize, envision,* or *picture.* Remind students that the leads should hook the reader and relate to the remainder of the text. Invite students to share their original and revised leads. Which one is more engaging?

Begin with a Verb

1. Before beginning this lesson, you may need to review verbs and the roles verbs play in sentences.

   • Reread the following sentence from "The Corn Palace":

   "Built in 1892 in Mitchell, South Dakota, the Corn Palace was created to dramatically display the products of the harvest of South Dakota's farmers, in murals on the outside of the building."

2. Create a chart, such as the following:

stretch	stretching	stretched
name	naming	named
consider	considering	considered

3. Explain that writers sometimes use verbs to vary sentence beginnings. Model several examples:

   • *Stretching* their necks to the tops of trees, giraffes access food that is out of reach for most animals.

   • *Named* after the king of the Roman gods, Jupiter has a surface temperature of -108 °C.

   • *Considered* one of five top natural resources, forests play a pivotal role in our complex ecosystem.

   As Jeff Anderson (2005) explains, each opener introduces a complete sentence. Test this out in the sentences above. Is there an "opener" followed by a complete sentence? Writers signal "openers" by inserting a comma at the end of each one.

4. With students' help, use other words, such as *accept, accepting, accepted; examine, examining, examined; open, opening, opened; rest, resting, rested; reach, reaching, reached; gather, gathering, gathered;* and *harvest, harvesting, harvested,* to generate additional sentences that begin with participles. Ideally, students should generate sentences based on content they are studying in science or social studies.

Building Bridges Between Ideas

1. Reread "The Corn Palace," and then call students' attention to how the author used words to move from one sentence to another.

   - In lines 1, 2, and 3, the author uses *a building*, *that same building* and *this building* to move the reader through the text.

   - In lines 4 and 5, the author uses the word *murals* near the end of one sentence and at the beginning of a new sentence. The repeated word provides a bridge between the sentences.

   - In lines 9–12, the author listed the types of grains and grasses in the murals, and in line 13, the author grouped the items together and called them *corn decorations*.

2. Using a different text, for example, Margriet Ruurs' (2005) "My Librarian is a Camel: How Books Are Brought to Children Around the World" (CCSS Appendix B, p. 72), have students circle or highlight the words the author uses to connect her ideas. Discuss how the words help the text flow together smoothly and help the reader understand it.

Extension

Invite students to reread one of their writing samples and identify words that link their sentences into a cohesive text. If students have not used words to bridge ideas, conference with them or arrange a small group to examine where they might repeat a key word or categorize words to create a cohesive text.

Why/How Organization

1. Return to "The Corn Palace" and highlight the section of the article in which the author explains *why* the palace was built. Using a different colored marker (or sticky note), identify the section of the text that explains *how* it was built. (*Why* it is built is described in lines 6–8 , and *how* it is built is described in lines 9–14.)

2. Using a different text that follows this *Why/How* pattern, perhaps "The Evolution of the Grocery Bag" (CCSS Appendix B, 98), ask students to work with a partner to highlight (with a marker or sticky notes) the section in which the author explains why square-bottom grocery bags were needed. Using a different colored marker (or sticky note), have them identify the section of the text that explains how they were made.

3. If students are not able to apply this strategy to their writing immediately, take a few minutes to brainstorm some possible topics that lend themselves to this organizational pattern (e.g., how and why an airplane was invented or the telephone, water coolers, and scooters).

Mentor Text: "Louis' Lunch"

Louis' Lunch
A Local Legacy
(from Library of Congress)

Do you love hamburgers? Do you know how they were created?

The first hamburgers in U.S. history were served in New Haven, Connecticut, at Louis' Lunch sandwich shop in 1895. Louis Lassen, founder of Louis' Lunch, ran a small lunch wagon selling steak sandwiches to local factory workers. Because he didn't like to waste the excess beef from his daily lunch rush, he ground it up, grilled it, and served it between two slices of bread—and America's first hamburger was created.

The small Crown Street luncheonette is still owned and operated by third and fourth generations of the Lassen family. Hamburgers are still the specialty of the house, where steak is ground fresh each day and hand molded, slow cooked, broiled vertically, and served between two slices of toast with your choice of only three "acceptable" garnishes: cheese, tomato, and onion.

Want ketchup or mustard? Forget it. You will be told "no" in no uncertain terms. This is the home of the greatest hamburger in the world, claim the owners, who are perhaps best known for allowing their customers to have a burger the "Lassen way" or not at all.

Additional Thoughts:
What do you wonder? What did you discover? What do you want to discuss?

Sample Jottings: "Louis' Lunch"

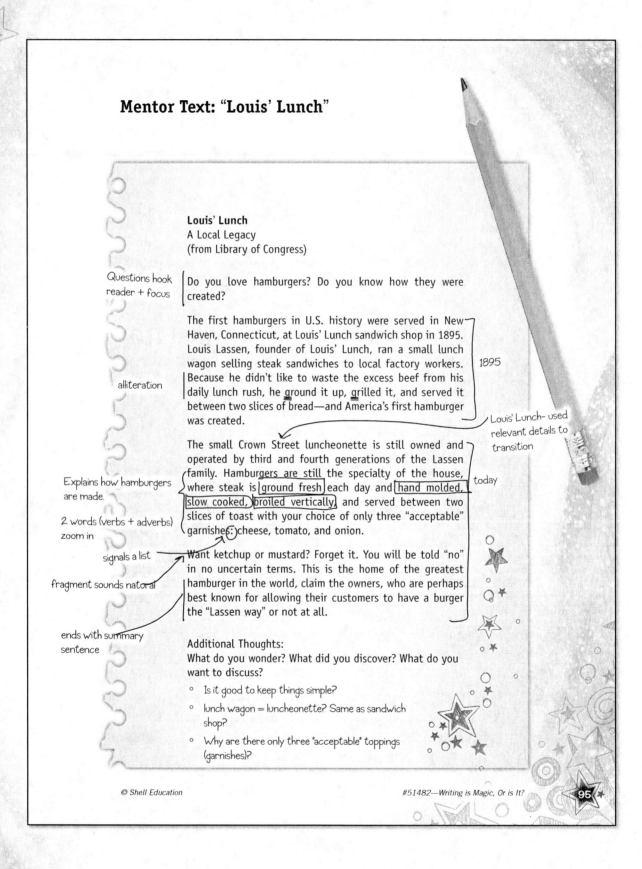

Mentor Text: "Louis' Lunch"

Louis' Lunch
A Local Legacy
(from Library of Congress)

Questions hook reader + focus — Do you love hamburgers? Do you know how they were created?

alliteration — The first hamburgers in U.S. history were served in New Haven, Connecticut, at Louis' Lunch sandwich shop in 1895. Louis Lassen, founder of Louis' Lunch, ran a small lunch wagon selling steak sandwiches to local factory workers. Because he didn't like to waste the excess beef from his daily lunch rush, he ground it up, grilled it, and served it between two slices of bread—and America's first hamburger was created. *1895*

Louis' Lunch- used relevant details to transition

Explains how hamburgers are made.

2 words (verbs + adverbs) zoom in — The small Crown Street luncheonette is still owned and operated by third and fourth generations of the Lassen family. Hamburgers are still the specialty of the house, where steak is ground fresh each day and hand molded, slow cooked, broiled vertically, and served between two slices of toast with your choice of only three "acceptable" garnishes: cheese, tomato, and onion. *today*

signals a list

fragment sounds natural — Want ketchup or mustard? Forget it. You will be told "no" in no uncertain terms. This is the home of the greatest hamburger in the world, claim the owners, who are perhaps best known for allowing their customers to have a burger the "Lassen way" or not at all.

ends with summary sentence

Additional Thoughts:
What do you wonder? What did you discover? What do you want to discuss?

○ Is it good to keep things simple?
○ lunch wagon = luncheonette? Same as sandwich shop?
○ Why are there only three "acceptable" toppings (garnishes)?

Close Reading: "Louis' Lunch"

What does the text say?

The purpose of this section is to address students' comprehension and to focus on what the text says. Here, we model how to ask text-dependent questions in order to encourage students to infer meaning.

> **Close reading** is "an instructional routine in which students critically examine a text, especially through repeated readings" (Fisher and Frey 2012, 179). Using a short passage, students read carefully to determine what the text says and to uncover specific instances of the author's craft, including items such as word choice, sentence structure, endings, leads, and more.

1. Kick off this close read by asking: Why do you think the author of "Louis' Lunch" began with the two questions he or she raised? What do you expect to learn about in this text, based on the two questions in the first paragraph? Students may say that the author began with two questions to hook the reader. The questions invite readers into the text and also add voice to the piece. Readers may anticipate that this text will be about how hamburgers were created.

2. What does the author want us to know about Louis' Lunch? What did the text say? Accept all evidence-based responses.

3. Each paragraph plays a specific role. The first paragraph let us know what the essay will be about. Turn and talk: What is the gist of the second paragraph? What is the big idea (or ideas) the author wants us to understand? Have a few students share their thoughts. Once the author's intended meaning is clear, repeat this process with the third paragraph and then the final paragraph.

4. The author calls Louis' Lunch a *sandwich shop*. Later, the author uses two other terms that mean nearly the same as *sandwich shop*. What terms does the author use? (*lunch wagon, luncheonette*)

5. At the end of the third paragraph, the author uses the word *garnish*. What does this word mean? What three garnishes are available at Louis' Lunch? Why do you think the owners only allow three toppings? (*That is the "Lassen way."*) What information in the text led you to this conclusion? (*the final paragraph*)

6. What word in the last paragraph lets you know that the owners of Louis' Lunch think it is the home of the greatest hamburger in the world, but that others may disagree? (*The author used the words "claim the owners."*)

How does the text say it?

In this section, we point out some of the strategies the author of "Louis' Lunch" used to craft this text. In the lessons that follow, you and your students will learn more about the strategies and how to integrate them into your own writing.

1. Either separate students into three "focus" groups and have each group investigate one of the following topics or keep the whole group intact and have all students zoom in on the use of adverbs to add detail, the use of the colon to signal a list, and the conclusion—what did the author do to create it? (The following notes will provide guidance for these three topics.)

2. Recap what students discovered about the author's craft, and then initiate a close read to continue an analysis of the writing.

3. Students may have noticed the alliteration in the second paragraph (*he ground it up, grilled it...*). In the third paragraph, the author moves away from alliteration, but focuses instead on pairing verbs and adverbs (*ground fresh, hand molded, slow cooked, broiled vertically*). Read the sentence as the author composed it, and reread a second time, omitting the adverbs. (*Hamburgers are still the specialty of the house, where steak is ground each day, molded, cooked, and broiled.*)

   • Discuss how each adverb in the original sentence provided a level of specificity. The adverbs help the reader picture exactly how the steak was ground, made into patties, and then cooked.

4. Next, invite students to share what they know about the function of a colon as used in the last sentence of the third paragraph. If students are not familiar with this punctuation mark, explain that it is used to signal a list. The Owlet website (Online Writing and Learning at LeTourneau University), explains, "A colon says that you have introduced what will follow. Think of a colon as a pair of eyes, looking ahead to what's coming next" (http://owlet.letu.edu/ grammarlinks/punctuation/punct2d.html). Go back to check the use of the colon in "Louis' Lunch." Does it serve as a pair of eyes looking ahead at what is to come?

5. Finally, as you reread the concluding sentence, discuss the word *claim*. Ask: what does *claim* mean in this sentence? Students may know that a claim is a statement that someone asserts is true. The statement can often be disputed. What claim did the owners of Louis' Lunch make?

Extension

Discuss some other claims that could (or should not) be made based on the information in the article (e.g., Louis Lassen was a practical man. Louis' Lunch has been a family-owned business for over 200 years. Louis' Lunch has expanded to be one of New Haven's largest hamburger spots. Customers at Louis' Lunch shouldn't expect to find hamburger rolls.).

Zooming In: Analyzing Writing Strategies

Here are three strategies the author used. You can also implement these with your students by following the suggested lesson ideas below.

1. **Adding Details with Adverbs:** This strategy focuses on using adverbs to tell why, how, when, and under what condition something is happening or has happened. The author of "Louis' Lunch" used adverbs to add information about the process used to make hamburgers. The meat is *ground fresh*, *hand molded*, *slow cooked*, and *broiled vertically*. If the author chose not to include the

adverbs, readers would know what happened—the meat was ground, molded, cooked, and broiled, but they would not know how each step was completed (e.g., ground *fresh, hand* molded).

2. **Why a Colon?:** Colons often signal a list, which is the grammar generalization introduced in this strategy. In Louis's Lunch there are *only three "acceptable" garnishes: cheese, tomato, and onion.*

3. **Concluding with a Claim:** A claim is what someone believes to be true. "Conclude with a Claim" enables writers to bring closure to an informative text by stating one (*indisputable*) truth about the topic. It is clear from the final sentence in "Louis' Lunch" that the luncheonette owners truly believe their restaurant is home to the greatest hamburger in the world.

Lesson Ideas: "Louis' Lunch"

Once you and your students have identified instances of author's craft, we believe it is important to name the strategies and to empower students to try out the strategies in their own writing. These lesson ideas provide you with opportunities for your students to practice the strategies with support from you and their peers.

Adding Details with Adverbs

1. In preparation for this lesson, have students collect pictures of dogs from magazines, grocery store circulars, the internet, or their own photos. They will use them in this lesson to generate verbs and adverbs.

2. Begin by reading the sentence: "Hamburgers are still the specialty of the house, where steak is *ground fresh* each day and *hand molded, slow cooked, broiled vertically,* and *served* between two slices of toast with your choice of only three 'acceptable' garnishes: cheese, tomato, and onion."

3. Call students' attention to the verbs and adverbs (italics added above). Explain how adverbs help describe the verbs. Adverbs and adverbial phrases tell why, how, when, and under what condition something is happening or has happened.

4. In pairs, have students select an image from the dog pictures they collected. Ask them to brainstorm verbs and adverbs to go along with the photo. Encourage students to use precise, unanticipated (but relevant) adverbs. Model a couple of examples before sending the students off (e.g., panted softly, slept peacefully, and begged until he got food). Record your thoughts on an anchor chart. Add student examples at the end of the guided lesson when they share their work with the class.

Teachers often use chart paper to create **anchor charts** with their students. The charts capture and make visible important ideas from a lesson, procedures, and strategies that students may want to refer back to in the future.

Why a Colon?

1. Without yet revealing the generalization, show several examples of colons used to signal a list, and ask students if they can determine what convention or grammar rule is used in each example. You might want to use sentences, such as

   • The following three conditions must be in place for a blizzard to occur: snow, winds in excess of 35 mph, and reduced visibility (less than ¼ mile) for three consecutive hours.

   • President John F. Kennedy had two children: John F. Kennedy, Jr. and Caroline Kennedy.

   • Four states in the United States of America meet at a single point: Utah, Colorado, Arizona, and New Mexico.

   After students determine the rule, review each of the three sentences to see if the rule works.

2. Next, cut out a dozen or so pictures of items from a grocery flier or department store catalogue. Place the items in a paper bag. Have a student select four or five pictures and create a sentence following the pattern in today's lesson. Students should also be aware that colons are not used unless what comes before the colon is a complete sentence or includes the words *as follows* or *the following*.

   • For example, you would not need a colon in these two sentences:

   Monkeys like to eat fruits, such as bananas, blueberries, apples, and grapes.

   The four US states that meet at a single point are Utah, Colorado, Arizona, and New Mexico.

As you conference with students, encourage them to include this strategy in their informational writing and then share their examples with classmates.

Conclude with a Claim

1. Return to "Louis' Lunch" and focus on the conclusion. Point out the word *claim* and discuss what a claim is—something that you believe to be true. Discuss how the author used a claim as a way to bring closure to the piece. In essence, the author summarizes the text by proclaiming what he or she understands to be true.

   • Next, display Aliki's "My Five Senses" (CCSS Appendix B, 29). Read the text together and discuss the conclusion. Aliki does not use the word *claim*, but it is clear that she concludes with a claim (belief) that her senses are always working and that they make her aware of the world.

⋆Extension

> Using one of your pieces of writing, a student's piece of writing, or a published writing sample, talk through how this strategy could be used to draft or revise a conclusion for it.

Mentor Text: "Bean-Hole Beans"

Bean-Hole Beans
A Local Legacy
(from Library of Congress)

What's a bean-hole bean? No, it's not a bean with a hole in it. Bean-hole beans get their name because they are baked in a hole. For hundreds of years, the Penobscot Indians of Maine cooked their food in a hole in the ground. The first thing you need to cook bean-hole beans is a shovel!

Recipe for bean-hole beans:

-Dig a hole in the ground 3 feet deep and line it with rocks.

-Build a fire in the hole and let it burn down to large embers and ash. (This can take half a day before enough coals are produced to cook the beans properly.)

-Use dry beans such as Great Northern, Yellow Eye, Jacob's Cattle, or Soldier.

-Other ingredients include onions, salt pork, ham hock, bacon, tomatoes, brown sugar and molasses.

Put the beans and other ingredients in a cast iron pot and cover with water and a lid. Place the pot in the hole, cover with a wet dish towel or burlap sack, shovel some of the embers and ashes on top of the pot, and then cover with dirt. Cooking time varies depending on which recipe is used but, it can take as long as 16 hours. Then get ready with a shovel and a bowl!

Additional Thoughts:
What do you wonder? What did you discover? What do you want to discuss?

Sample Jottings: "Bean-Hole Beans"

Mentor Text: "Bean-Hole Beans"

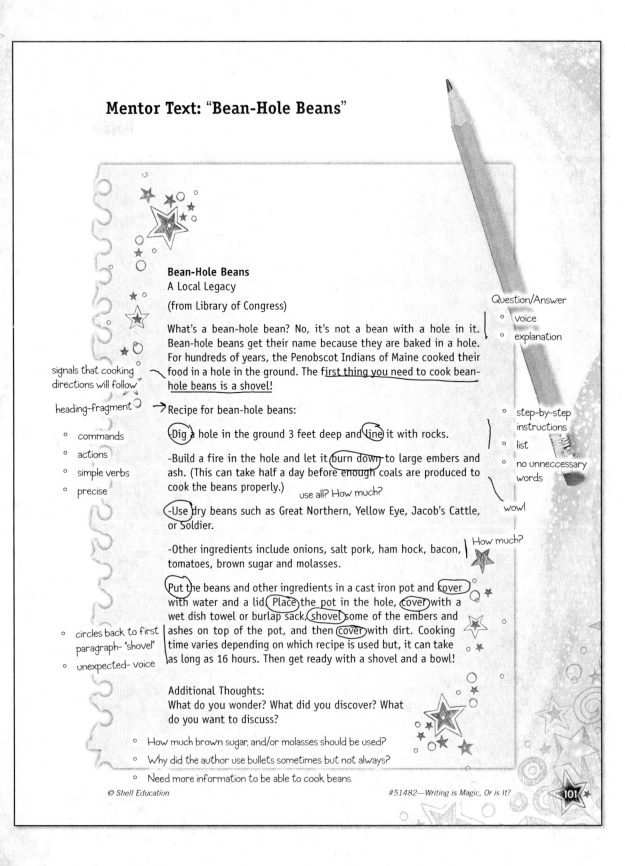

Bean-Hole Beans
A Local Legacy
(from Library of Congress)

What's a bean-hole bean? No, it's not a bean with a hole in it. Bean-hole beans get their name because they are baked in a hole. For hundreds of years, the Penobscot Indians of Maine cooked their food in a hole in the ground. The <u>first thing you need to cook bean-hole beans is a shovel!</u>

Recipe for bean-hole beans:

Dig a hole in the ground 3 feet deep and line it with rocks.

-Build a fire in the hole and let it burn down to large embers and ash. (This can take half a day before enough coals are produced to cook the beans properly.)

-Use dry beans such as Great Northern, Yellow Eye, Jacob's Cattle, or Soldier.

-Other ingredients include onions, salt pork, ham hock, bacon, tomatoes, brown sugar and molasses.

Put the beans and other ingredients in a cast iron pot and cover with water and a lid. Place the pot in the hole, cover with a wet dish towel or burlap sack, shovel some of the embers and ashes on top of the pot, and then cover with dirt. Cooking time varies depending on which recipe is used but, it can take as long as 16 hours. Then get ready with a shovel and a bowl!

Additional Thoughts:
What do you wonder? What did you discover? What do you want to discuss?

- How much brown sugar, and/or molasses should be used?
- Why did the author use bullets sometimes but not always?
- Need more information to be able to cook beans.

Handwritten annotations:

- signals that cooking directions will follow
- heading-fragment
  - commands
  - actions
  - simple verbs
  - precise
- circles back to first paragraph- "shovel"
- unexpected- voice

- Question/Answer
  - voice
  - explanation
- step-by-step instructions
- list
- no unneccessary words
- wow!
- use all? How much?
- How much?

© Shell Education   #51482—Writing is Magic, Or is It?   101

Close Reading: "Bean-Hole Beans"

What does the text say?

The purpose of this section is to address students' comprehension and to focus on what the text says. Here, we model how to ask text-dependent questions in order to encourage students to infer meaning.

> **Close reading** is "an instructional routine in which students critically examine a text, especially through repeated readings" (Fisher and Frey 2012, 179). Using a short passage, students read carefully to determine what the text says and to uncover specific instances of the author's craft, including items such as word choice, sentence structure, endings, leads, and more.

1. Ask students to read "Bean-Hole Beans" and jot down what they notice. Have them share some of their observations. If students do not mention the author's purpose, ask why the author wrote this article and how they determined its purpose. Students might suggest, for instance, that the author wrote this essay to explain how to cook bean-hole beans. The author's purpose is evident in the following sentences from the text: In the first paragraph, the author states, "The first thing you need to cook bean-hole beans is a shovel!" The next line reads, "Recipe for bean-hole beans."

2. Have students think about cooking the beans. The author lets readers know that it could take 16 hours to cook beans in a hole. According to the text, why might it take so long?

3. If you were to cook beans according to the directions in this recipe, what equipment, in addition to a shovel, would you need? What additional information could the author have included to make the steps clearer to follow? Your students may respond that they would need something to light the fire (e.g., matches) and a knife to cut the other ingredients. The author does not specify how many beans to use or the amount of *other ingredients* to add. To cook the beans, readers know they must *shovel some of the embers and ashes on top of the pot* but are not told how high to fill the hole. Students may come up with additional details to clarify this recipe.

4. Concentrate on the last sentence. Why would someone need a shovel and a bowl? Ask: Could you imagine yourself trying this recipe? Why or why not? Use information in the text to support your answer.

How does the text say it?

We now invite you to reveal the magician's magic and unpack how the writer crafted this text. Either separate students into three "focus" groups and have each group investigate one of the following topics or keep the whole group intact and have all students zoom in on the imperatives (verbs) used in the procedures, the text's organization (structure), or the conclusion.

1. Recap what students discovered about the writing of "Bean-Hole Beans" and then initiate a close read to continue the analysis of the writing.

2. Investigate the organizational structure. Say: When we look at how this text is organized, it looks and feels different from the other informational texts in this chapter. Turn and talk: How is this text organized, and how is it different from the other informational texts in this chapter? Students are likely to indicate that in addition to the purpose, the author includes ingredients or materials, steps (in the order in which they should be completed), and a conclusion.

    - If students are not already familiar with the basic elements of procedural writing, let them know that this text is characteristic of this genre. Sometimes authors write steps in a procedure in a numbered or bulleted list, other times the procedures appear in an essay format. In this case, the author begins with bullets and embeds steps in a paragraph.

3. Next, call attention to the verbs. As you read aloud, circle the first three or four imperative verbs, also known as "bossy verbs" (e.g., *dig, line,* and *build*), and then invite students to help you circle the remaining imperative verbs. Discuss the use of imperatives in procedural writing (i.e., why an author would use them) and the effect they have on the pace of the writing. Your students may suggest that writers of procedural texts often use imperatives because they clearly show actions (e.g., *arrange, glue, locate, notice, blend*). The imperatives often, but not always, are placed in a prominent place at the beginning of sentences or lines in directions so they are easy to spot.

4. Finally, discuss the final sentence in the article. To whom is the author speaking? How does this sentence connect back to the first paragraph? Does the author's voice change from paragraph to paragraph? If so, where and how does it change? The author begins with a humorous voice to hook the reader and then switches to a series of straightforward commands (imperative verbs) when explaining the procedures used to cook the beans. In the final sentence, after all directions have been listed, the author reverts back to a humorous voice to conclude the text.

○ Zooming In: Analyzing Writing Strategies

Here are three strategies the author used. You can also implement these with your students by following the suggested lesson ideas below.

1. **Imperatives:** This strategy offers writers opportunities to add specificity to their texts by calling attention to imperatives (or "bossy verbs"). When making bean-hole beans, the author used precise verbs, such as *dig, line, build,* and *place*.

2. **"How-To" Organization:** "How-to" texts generally follow a recognizable organizational formula, which includes a purpose, ingredients or materials, step-by-step instructions, and a conclusion.

3. **Ta-Da!:** Often the conclusion of a procedural piece of writing contains a statement that applauds the reader for successfully completing the directions. The "Ta-Da!" strategy encourages writers to show excitement and conclude with a bit of fanfare. "Bean-Hole Beans" concluded with a jovial announcement: "Then get ready with a shovel and a bowl!"—a true Ta-da moment!

Lesson Ideas: "Bean-Hole Beans"

Once you and your students have identified instances of author's craft, we believe it is important to name the strategies and to empower students to try out the strategies in their own writing. These lesson ideas provide you with opportunities for your students to practice the strategies with support from you and their peers.

Imperatives

1. This lesson is designed to help students begin to think about precise, specific, concrete verbs for procedural writing. Begin by assigning a how-to task, one that students may actually carry out (e.g., creating a storyboard or a digital story) or one that they may simply plan (e.g., how to build a picture frame or create a class mural).

2. Explain the task and arrange students into small groups. Give students time to brainstorm the precise verbs and steps they would use to complete the task. As you circulate around, challenge students to replace common or vague verbs (e.g., *get, find, make, put*) with precise words. Precise verbs provide additional information for readers. You might encourage a student who writes *get some food* to use a more precise imperative, such as *purchase, prepare, cook*. Of course, the precise verb will need to be appropriate for the context. Instead of *make a picture*, writers might say *draw, quickly sketch*, or *copy*. Once complete, have students share their writing. Discuss the variation in word choice and the impact of each choice on how the task may be completed.

3. Review this lesson throughout the year as opportunities for authentic procedure writing become available.

How-to Organization

1. Unveil the structure of "Bean-Hole Beans" by highlighting each element of procedural writing with a different color marker. Have students identify the author's purpose and highlight it. Continue with ingredients/materials and highlight them in a different color. When students identify the verbs, highlight them in a third color. Finally, highlight the conclusion in a fourth color. Once complete, review features of the organizational structure that made this recipe easy for the reader to follow and features (or missing features) that made it challenging.

2. Next, take a look at "Vermont Maple Syrup" (http://www.americaslibrary.gov/es/vt/es_vt_syrup_1.html). In this article, the directions for making maple syrup are

If possible, it is best to teach **procedural writing** when you and your students have an authentic purpose and audience for the task. Procedures might be written to someone who will take care of a class pet or plant, or to help someone locate hard-to-find places in the building. Moreover, you may find authentic purposes for writing procedures by asking members of the local community for suggestions. Some citizens, for example, may want to learn how to move photos from a smart phone or tablet to an online image publishing service, or new parents might welcome directions for reading a book aloud to a young child.

written within an essay. With students' help, repeat the process you just used earlier with "Bean-Hole Beans," highlighting the different elements of this genre with different colors. Use a bulleted list format to rewrite the directions in "Vermont Maple Syrup."

3. If students have a piece of procedural writing, have them highlight the various elements. If not, engage students in an authentic procedural writing experience (e.g., how to use the self-service kiosks at your local post office, how to video record with a smartphone, or for young children, how to call 911 in an emergency) and guide them through the elements of a "how-to" organization pattern.

Conclusion: Ta-da!

1. Often the conclusion of a procedural piece of writing contains a statement that applauds the reader for successfully completing the directions. The writer usually shows excitement and sometimes concludes with a bit of fanfare. With students, reread the final sentence in "Bean-Hole Beans," and discuss why the author used "Ta-da!" to bring closure to this text. Next, look at the conclusion of Gibbons "From Seed to Plant" (CCSS Appendix B, 54). Discuss what the writer expects the reader to do after meeting with success: *water them… and watch them grow.*

2. Look at conclusions from other procedural writing samples. Many examples can be found online by typing *samples of procedural writing* in your search engine. Talk about whether or not the examples you selected contain conclusions and if so, whether or not the conclusions provided effective closure. Have students identify samples that end with clear, strong voices and the fanfare of "Ta-da" conclusions.

3. Finally, return to a piece of procedural writing that you and/or your students have written (or one you found online) and revise it to include a "Ta-da!" conclusion.

Reflection Questions

1. In Chapter 1, we talked about writers as writers and readers. How can you use your students' "jottings" to enhance this reader-writer relationship?

2. What can we learn about informational writing by looking within each mentor text and across the mentor texts in this chapter?

Chapter 5

Narrative Nonfiction Writing

Narrative nonfiction, also referred to as creative nonfiction and literary nonfiction, is a relatively new genre that merges literary art and research nonfiction.

> The words 'creative' and 'nonfiction' describe the form. The word 'creative' refers to the use of literary craft, the techniques fiction writers, playwrights, and poets employ to present nonfiction—factually accurate prose about real people and events—in a compelling, vivid, dramatic manner. The goal is to make nonfiction stories read like fiction so that your readers are as enthralled by fact as they are by fantasy (Gutkind 2012, under "Issue #0 What is Creative Nonfiction").

Described in a slightly different way, "...creative nonfiction uses literary styles and techniques to communicate facts and true stories. In contrast to technical writing and journalistic writing, creative nonfiction reads like a short story or novel, but unlike fiction the story is true" (Spence 2011, under "Types of Writing: What is Creative Nonfiction").

Narrative nonfiction includes memoirs and biographies; travel, sports, science and nature writing; and personal essays. In this genre, the personality of the writer is apparent in his or her reactions, reflections, and interpretations of the events, places, ideas or lives of the subjects. As Jenny Spinner (2004) put it, "Thus, not only do we use 'personal presence' to define the genre of creative nonfiction, we use it to define creative nonfiction against other genres (poetry, fiction, drama) and against the umbrella genre of nonfiction" (317). Creative nonfiction goes beyond traditional nonfiction that might convey or summarize information and shows the writer's knowledge, thoughts, and feelings.

Since the genre of narrative nonfiction melds elements of informative/explanatory writing and narrative writing, both are addressed here. The previous chapter contains a chart that depicts the writing skills and understandings for information writing that students in grades 3–8 are expected to demonstrate. If you look at the Common Core State Standards (CCSS) for narrative writing, you will see how they align with narrative nonfiction. For instance, Standard 4.3 asks fourth graders to write narratives to "develop real or imagined experiences or events using effective technique, descriptive details, and clear event sequences." Additionally, the standards discuss using "dialogue and description to develop experiences and events..." (CCSS.ELA-Literacy.W.4.3b), to "use a variety of transitional words and phrases to manage the sequence of events"

(CCSS.ELA-Literacy.W.4.3c), to "use concrete words and phrases and sensory details to convey experiences and events precisely" (CCSS.ELA-Literacy.W.4.3d), and to "provide a conclusion that follows from the narrated experiences or events" (CCSS.ELA-Literacy.W4.3e).

Thomas Newkirk (2012) contends, "narrative is the deep structure of all good writing" (29) and that nonfiction writers do not abandon narration, but rather they "use narrative in more complex and embedded ways" (32). Lucy Calkins, Mary Ehrenworth, and Christopher Lehman (2012), too, emphasize commonalities across genres. They explain, for example, that writers of argument, information, and narration must include effective beginnings and conclusions that tie together and bring closure to a text. All writers, regardless of genre, need to elaborate.

Narrative nonfiction provides writers with opportunities to observe how these common elements are used effectively in this genre and then apply their understandings in creative ways.

Writing Strategies Used in Narrative Nonfiction

The samples in this chapter model the artful use of specific craft strategies. Through close reading, we identify the following writing strategies, and we discuss how the writer uses strategies to communicate and enhance the meaning of the writing.

You will find a clean "student copy" of each mentor text in Appendix B. If you think your students will be able to understand, or at least get the gist of the text on their own, begin by providing them with copies of the text, have them read it independently (or with a partner), and annotate it as they read. In their jottings, they should note text features (e.g., italicized words, headings, and key words), interesting or unfamiliar use of language, the organizational structure of the text, questions the text raises for them, author's craft (e.g., alliteration, metaphor, varied sentence constructions, effective leads, transitions, and conclusions). If you think the text may be too challenging for your students to comprehend independently, distribute the clean copy and then engage in a guided close read. (See the next two sections for guidance.)

Once students have read and annotated the text (i.e., completed their "jottings"), call them together into a large group to discuss the content of the text (i.e., *What* does the text say?) and then to investigate how the author crafted the text (i.e., *How* does the text say it?). Rather than share our sample jottings directly with your students, we envision that you will use our annotations to help guide your students through the close readings.

Factual Information vs. the Author's Personal Response/Reaction/Reflections:
This strategy helps writers differentiate between facts (truths) and opinions that authors of narrative nonfiction typically integrate into their texts.

Voice, Tone, and Mood: With this strategy, we explore how writers of narrative nonfiction achieve a voice, tone, and mood that are characteristic of this genre.

Coordinating Conjunctions (FANBOYS): *For, And, Nor, But, Or, Yet,* and *So* are coordinating conjunctions that link two independent clauses (i.e., complete sentences). Commas are generally used with each conjunction to separate the clauses.

White Space: Writers must decide whether to indent paragraphs or leave white spaces between paragraphs. Either style is acceptable, but writers should not alternate between the two. In this strategy, we explore the purposes of creating paragraphs in written texts.

Fulfilling a Promise: This strategy, created by Muriel Harris (as cited in McAndrew and Reigstad 2001, 44), points to the fact that authors make a promise to readers to write about one topic or thesis. Students determine what promise an author makes and evaluate how parts of the text help fulfill the promise.

Word Choice—Strong Verbs: In this strategy, we explore strong verbs and why they are important in narrative nonfiction writing.

Mentor Text: "The Peanut Man"

The Peanut Man
A Local Legacy
(from Library of Congress)

George Washington Carver was always interested in plants. When he was a child, he was known as the "plant doctor." He had a secret garden where he grew all kinds of plants. People would ask him for advice when they had sick plants. Sometimes he'd take their plants to his garden and nurse them back to health. (paragraph 1)

Later, when he was teaching at Tuskegee Institute, he put his plant skills to good use. Many people in the South had been growing only cotton on their land. Cotton plants use most of the nutrients in the soil. (Nutrients provide nourishment to plants.) So the soil becomes "worn out" after a few years. Eventually, cotton will no longer grow on this land. (paragraph 2)

This was especially bad for poor African American farmers, who relied on selling cotton to support themselves. Carver was dedicated to helping those farmers, so he came up with a plan. (paragraph 3)

Carver knew that certain plants put nutrients back into the soil. One of those plants is the peanut! Peanuts are also a source of protein. (paragraph 4)

Carver thought that if those farmers planted peanuts, the plants would help restore their soil, provide food for their animals, and provide protein for their families—quite a plant! In 1896 peanuts were not even recognized as a crop in the United States, but Carver would help change that. (paragraph 5)

#51482—Writing is Magic, Or Is It?

Carver told farmers to rotate their crops: plant cotton one year, then the next year plant peanuts and other soil-restoring plants, like peas and sweet potatoes. It worked! The peanut plants grew and produced lots of peanuts. The plants added enough nutrients to the soil so cotton grew the next year. Now the farmers had lots of peanuts—too many for their families and animals—and no place to sell the extras. Again, Carver had a plan. Do you know what he did? (paragraph 6)

Carver invented all kinds of things made out of peanuts. He wrote down more than 300 uses for peanuts, including peanut milk, peanut paper, and peanut soap. Carver thought that if farmers started making things out of peanuts, they'd have to buy fewer things and would be more self-sufficient. And if other people started making things out of peanuts, they would want to buy the extra peanuts, so the farmers would make more money. Although not many of Carver's peanut products were ever mass-produced, he did help spread the word about peanuts. (paragraph 7)

Peanuts became more and more popular. By 1920 there were enough peanut farmers to form the United Peanut Association of America (UPAA). In 1921 the UPAA asked Carver to speak to the U.S. Congress about the many uses for peanuts. Soon the whole country had heard of George Washington Carver, the Peanut Man! And by 1940 peanuts had become one of the top six crops in the U.S. (paragraph 8)

Additional Thoughts:
What do you wonder? What did you discover? What do you want to discuss?

Sample Jottings: "The Peanut Man"

Mentor Text: "The Peanut Man"

The Peanut Man
A Local Legacy
(from Library of Congress)

main idea → George Washington Carver was always interested in plants. When
he was a child, he was known as the "plant doctor." He had a
facts — secret garden where he grew all kinds of plants. People would
ask him for advice when they had sick plants. Sometimes he'd
take their plants to his garden and nurse them back to health.
(paragraph 1)

*Quotation marks show
words are used in unusual
ways. Carver wasn't a real
doctor and the soil wasn't
really worn out.*

main idea → Later, when he was teaching at Tuskegee Institute, he put his
plant skills to good use. Many people in the South had been
Explanation growing only cotton on their land. Cotton plants use most of the
nutrients in the soil. (Nutrients provide nourishment to plants.) So
Problem #1 the soil becomes "worn out" after a few years. Eventually, cotton
will no longer grow on this land. (paragraph 2)

This was especially bad for poor African American farmers,
transition who relied on selling cotton to support themselves. Carver was *FANBOYS*
dedicated to helping those farmers, [so] he came up with a plan.
(paragraph 3)

Carver knew that certain plants put nutrients back into the soil.
One of those plants is the peanut! Peanuts are also a source of
protein. (paragraph 4)

Solution #1 Carver thought that if those farmers planted peanuts, the
plants would help restore their soil, provide food for their
animals, and provide protein for their families—(quite a *Writer's*
plant!) In 1896 peanuts were not even recognized as a crop *reaction*
in the United States, [but] Carver would help change that.
(paragraph 5) *FANBOYS*

Problem #2

Carver told farmers to rotate their crops: plant cotton one year, then the next year plant peanuts and other soil-restoring plants, like peas and sweet potatoes. (It worked!) The peanut plants grew and produced lots of peanuts. The plants added enough nutrients to the soil so cotton grew the next year. Now the farmers had lots of peanuts—too many for their families and animals—and no place to sell the extras. Again, Carver had a plan. Do you know what he did? (paragraph 6)

Writer's reaction

transition

Question used to engage reader

Solution #2

Carver invented all kinds of things made out of peanuts. He wrote down more than 300 uses for peanuts, including peanut milk, peanut paper, and peanut soap. Carver thought that if farmers started making things out of peanuts, they'd have to buy fewer things and would be more self-sufficient. And if other people started making things out of peanuts, they would want to buy the extra peanuts, so the farmers would make more money. Although not many of Carver's peanut products were ever mass-produced, he did help spread the word about peanuts. (paragraph 7)

Peanut doctor in 1st paragraph and Peanut Man! in last paragraph.

Peanuts became more and more popular. By 1920 there were enough peanut farmers to form the United Peanut Association of America (UPAA). In 1921 the UPAA asked Carver to speak to the U.S. Congress about the many uses for peanuts. Soon the whole country had heard of George Washington Carver, the Peanut Man! And by 1940 peanuts had become one of the top six crops in the U.S. (paragraph 8)

Additional Thoughts:
What do you wonder? What did you discover? What do you want to discuss?

- How long did it take for peanuts to go from not being recognized as a crop to one of the top size crops in the US?

- Preanuts are very important plants.

- I wonder what would have happened if George Washington Carver never came up with a plan to help farmers.

Close Reading: "The Peanut Man"

What does the text say?

The purpose of this section is to address students' comprehension and to focus on what the text says. Here, we model how to ask text-dependent questions in order to encourage students to infer meaning.

> **Close reading** is "an instructional routine in which students critically examine a text, especially through repeated readings" (Fisher and Frey 2012, 179). Using a short passage, students read carefully to determine what the text says and to uncover specific instances of the author's craft, including items such as word choice, sentence structure, endings, leads, and more.

1. Before beginning to investigate how the author of "The Peanut Man" crafted this piece, spend a few minutes making sure students comprehend the text. Ask them to share what they noted in their "jottings" and then use the subsequent questions, or those you create, to extend their understandings.

2. Direct students' attention back to the first paragraph and discuss what it means to "nurse them [plants] back to health."

3. You may want to check in to make sure students understand what *nutrients* means (paragraphs 2 and 4) by asking: Do people need nutrients? How do people get the nutrients they need? (Answer: food, water/drinks, vitamins) Make sure students understand that the nutrients in what living organisms eat and drink help them grow and have energy to survive. Ask: Which of the following items would not be a nutrient for dogs: water, a healthy walk, or meat?

4. Continuing on, ask students to reread paragraph 6 and identify what plants the author is referring to in the fourth sentence ["The plants added enough nutrients to the soil…"]. You may want to check for comprehension by asking: Did George Washington Carver want cotton farmers to eliminate cotton crops and grow only peanuts? Explain. Why would it not be a good idea to grow only peanuts?

5. Reread paragraph seven and ask: If George Washington Carver's plan worked, how would peanut crops help farmers live better lives? Students may state, for instance, that farmers may need to rely less on other people ("be more self-sufficient") and farmers would have more income from the sale of peanut products. In pairs or small groups, have students reread paragraphs five and eight and calculate how long it took for peanuts to evolve from not being recognized as a crop to one of the top six crops in the United States. (Answer: 1940 – 1896 = 44 years)

6. Conclude the discussion with the following two questions: What did the text *tell* you about George Washington Carver? (The text *tells* us, for instance, that peanuts can help restore nutrients to the soil and that George Washington Carver knew this.) What did it *show* you about the type of person he was? (It *shows* us that Carver was passionate about helping farmers, especially poor African American farmers.)

How does the text say it?

Once students understand the author's intended message, it is time to look closely at the writer's craft. As you guide students through this read, you will help them differentiate between factual information and the author's personal response/reaction/reflections; then investigate how the author created voice, tone, and mood; and finally, introduce or review coordinating conjunctions (FANBOYS). This close read is designed to call attention to the author's craft. In the following three lessons, you'll teach students how to replicate these strategies.

1. If students have not already identified the following characteristic, point it out: "The Peanut Man" follows a problem/solution structure that we sometimes see in nonfiction writing, but it also reads like a story, which makes it a wonderful mentor text for the narrative nonfiction genre.

2. Begin by rereading or having students reread the first paragraph and ask them to identify its main idea and the factual details that support the main idea. Use a highlighter to mark the facts your students notice as they report out their thinking. Repeat this same process with the second paragraph. Ask: Why do you think the author chose to include these facts? What do they tell us and show us about George Washington Carver?

3. Next, have students reread the third paragraph. Ask what fact(s) they found and have them share their fact(s) with a partner. Continue to highlight the facts.

4. Move to the fourth paragraph. Ask: What three facts are included? (Each sentence contains one fact.) Contrast this with the information in paragraph five in which the first sentence contains three facts. Ask: How did combining all three facts into one sentence change the pace of the writing?

   • Next, call students' attention to "quite a plant!" by highlighting it with a different color marker. Ask: Is this a fact? Talk about the difference between this personal reaction and a fact (a truth) and initiate a discussion about why the author included a personal reaction. What impact did it have on the writing? How about on the relationship between reader and writer? Emphasize that the inclusion of personal reactions/reflections/responses is not only permissible in narrative nonfiction, it is expected.

   • Continue to highlight several facts and one additional personal reaction in the remainder of the text. Students may be able to identify "It worked!" as the writer response.

5. When ready, introduce voice, tone, and mood. We know that purpose, audience, and the topic of a piece of writing greatly influences voice, tone, and mood. You might want to initiate a discussion with the following questions: Why did the writer compose this essay? What was his/her purpose and for whom might this essay have been written? How would you describe the tone and mood (serious, lighthearted, funny, carefree, informative, formal, informal, whimsical, humorous, friendly, or dramatic)? Was this an appropriate tone and mood given the topic? Explain.

6. Next, draw students' attention back to the two places in the text where the author inserted his/her personal reaction (paragraphs five and six). Review how they contributed to the voice, tone, and mood the author established. Point out, or have students identify, other places where words and sentences reinforce the author's voice (e.g., the question at the end of paragraph six).

   - Take this opportunity to reiterate the difference between nonfiction and narrative nonfiction by asking students what this essay might "sound" like if it were a research paper. Students may suggest, for instance, that more technical terms may be used in a research paper, perhaps instead of "worn out," and specific details may be included. Instead of "The peanut plants grew and produced lots of peanuts," a research report may include numbers to support this claim. Continue by asking: What did the use of the narrative nonfiction genre allow the writer to do that he or she may not have been able to do if it were written as a more traditional nonfiction report? (See introduction to this chapter for a comparison between the two genres.)

7. Finally, have students take a moment to look at the conventions the author used. Display the following two sentences from the text and ask students to share what they notice about the use of punctuation.

   - Carver was dedicated to helping those farmers, so he came up with a plan.

   - In 1896 peanuts were not even recognized as a crop in the United States, but Carver would help change that.

     Guide students to see that the comma separates two complete sentences (independent clauses). Students may recall the acronym FANBOYS (for, and, nor, but, or, yet, so) and the convention that accompanies it. If not, do not worry about it. We will focus on FANBOYS in one of the following lessons. At this point, see if students can express how the comma makes it easier for the reader to understand the author's intended message.

8. Before concluding this close read, acknowledge that in the first paragraph the author refers to Carver as the "plant doctor," and in the final paragraph as the "Peanut Man!" Ask: What did you notice about the way these words were written (within quotation marks and lower-case letters vs. the two upper-case letters and an exclamation point)? How did the author use text features to convey his or her impression of George Washington Carver?

○ Zooming In: Analyzing Writing Strategies

Here are three strategies the author used. You can also implement these with your students by following the suggested lesson ideas below.

1. **Factual Information vs. the Author's Personal Response/ Reaction/ Reflections:** This strategy helps writers differentiate between facts (truths) and opinions that authors of narrative nonfiction typically integrate into their texts. Nutritionists have shown, for instance, *that peanuts are a source of protein,* so

this truth is a fact. When the author wrote, *quite a plant* (para. 5), however, he is providing a personal response/reaction/reflection/opinion.

2. **Voice, Tone, and Mood:** With this strategy, we explore how writers of narrative nonfiction achieve a voice, tone, and mood that are characteristic of this genre. The author's attitude towards his or her subject, which is often reflected in his or her voice, tone, and mood, can be revealed through word choice, language, sentence structure, details, dialogue, and description. Phrases such as *...he came up with a plan* and *It worked!* make evident the admiration the author feels for George Washington Carver.

3. **Coordinating Conjunctions (FANBOYS):** *For, And, Nor, But, Or, Yet,* and *So* are coordinating conjunctions that link two independent clauses (i.e., complete sentences). Commas are generally used with each conjunction to separate the clauses, as is the case in the following sentence *Carver was dedicated to helping those farmers, so he came up with a plan* (para. 3).

Lesson Ideas: "The Peanut Man"

Once you and your students have identified instances of author's craft, we believe it is important to name the strategies and to empower students to try out the strategies in their own writing. These lesson ideas provide you with opportunities for your students to practice the strategies with support from you and their peers.

Facts vs. Responses, Reactions, and Reflections

1. First, prepare students to think about facts vs. an author's personal response/ reaction/reflections by modeling this distinction with "The Peanut Man." If you followed the suggestions for the close read above, you probably highlighted the facts with one color highlighter and the reactions/reflections with a different color. Display your highlighted text and recap that (1) responses, reactions, and reflections reveal what the author is thinking and feeling; and (2) they enhance the personal presence of the writer, thereby intensifying a connection among the topic, writer, and reader.

2. Arrange students in pairs or small groups so they can *try on* the process you just modeled. Distribute a text that contains facts and responses/reactions/ reflections, such as Kathleen Kudlinski's "Boy, Were We Wrong About Dinosaurs" (for excerpt see ELA CCSS 2010 Appendix B, 55), and have students use two different colored highlighters (or create a two-column chart) to identify the facts and the author's responses/reactions/reflections.

3. As a whole class, discuss what students identified as facts and responses/ reactions/reflections.

4. Pose the following question: What did you learn from the author's responses/ reactions/reflections that you might not have learned if the piece were written as a traditional informational text?

Extension

Invite students to revisit a piece of narrative nonfiction they are writing (or have written). As they reread their texts, have students analyze their writing for facts vs. responses/reactions/reflections. If they have not included their personal presence through responses/reactions/reflections, ask them to do so and then share their revised copy with a classmate. Call upon a few students to articulate how the addition of the author's personal presence changed the quality of the writing.

Voice, Tone, Mood

1. Purpose, audience, and topic play an important role in determining the voice, tone, and mood of a piece (Mariconda 2014). Barbara Mariconda acknowledges that effective writers purposefully adjust their voices for their intended audiences, writing with a consistent word choice, tone, and style that will enable readers to access and learn from the informational text. Voice is the quality of writing through which authors convey their personalities. This lesson builds upon understandings from the previous lesson, namely that a distinguishing characteristic of narrative nonfiction is the author's strong presence. The author's attitude toward his or her subject, which is made known through voice, tone, and mood, can be revealed through word choice, language, sentence structure, details, dialogue, description, and the writer's effort to reach his or her reader.

Begin this lesson by displaying a T-chart that resembles the one that follows. Feel free to include additional features that contribute to voice, tone, or mood.

Feature	Example
Word choice (including strong verbs)	
Language	"…he came up with a plan" (para. 3)
Sentence structure (including fragments)	"It worked!" (para. 6)
Unique/interesting details	
Writer's effort to reach the reader	
Dialogue	
Description	

2. Reread "The Peanut Man" and model how you record evidence of voice, tone, and mood in the chart. Of course, not every piece of writing will contain every feature in the chart.

   • Invite students to add other examples to the chart by identifying features from other texts—for instance, "Boy, Were We Wrong About Dinosaurs," which was used in the lesson on facts vs. response/reactions/reflections (see prior lesson).

- Now that you have helped students discover the pigeons that were tucked up the sleeve of the narrative nonfiction "magician," have them practice enhancing voice, mood, or tone. Using one or more of the features identified in this lesson, ask students to revise one of their own texts, a published text of your choosing, or the following piece of writing:

Raccoons are mammals that weigh, on average, 24–38 pounds. They have black fur around their eyes, tails with five to eight alternating black and white rings on them, and quick paws. Raccoons easily adapt to their environments and eat a variety of food, including garbage that people leave behind. Raccoons do not hibernate, but they are seen less frequently in the winter because they often sleep in barns, trees, logs, and other resting spots for weeks at a time.

FANBOYS

1. *For, and, nor, but, or, yet, so* are coordinating conjunctions that link two complete sentences (two independent clauses). If there is an explicit subject and an explicit predicate on each side of the conjunction, a comma is generally used to separate the clauses.

   - Incorrect: Charlie washed his hands throughout the day, but caught his brother's cold anyway.

   - Correct: Charlie washed his hands throughout the day, but **he** caught his brother's cold anyway.

2. Call students' attention to two places in "The Peanut Man" where the author used this convention (paras. 3 and 5). Have students identify the subject and predicate of each clause. Provide additional examples and non-examples of FANBOYS. Have students decide if a comma is needed in each case, and explain why.

★Extension

- Independently, have students revise a piece of their writing by applying this convention and sharing their results.

- To stress the reader-writer connection, challenge students to find examples of FANBOYS in the texts they are reading. Create an anchor chart or a file in Dropbox to save their examples.

Note: Interestingly, when *so that* appears in a sentence, or is implied, writers do not generally use commas to separate clauses, as seen in paragraphs 6 and 7 of "The Peanut Man."

Mentor Text: "Confucius, the Great Chinese Philosopher"

Confucius, the Great Chinese Philosopher
Coan, Sharon, Jennifer Droll, and Kathleen C. Peterson.

In China long ago lived a man named Confucius. His teachings changed Chinese culture, and his influence continues today. Great thinkers called philosophers wondered about their laws and questioned, "Is this really right?" Confucius was one of these thinkers.

Confucius read many books that helped him think of ways in which his government could improve. He saw how the poor starved when the harvests failed. He watched the government abuse its power. Confucius wanted to help those in need, and he wanted to end wars. He devoted his life to this cause.

Confucius started a school and invited both nobles and peasants to learn. This was shocking. At that time, people believed that only nobles could be educated. Confucius knew that education could make people equal. His school was free. It had just one requirement: each student had to love learning.

Confucius taught his students that the government should help everyone have good lives. Rulers should earn their power through their concern for their people. He told his students to speak out against dishonest, corrupt rulers. It's not surprising that some rulers disliked him.

China would not be what it is today without Confucius's teachings. Other societies have followed his ideas as well. If Confucius were alive today, he would be amazed. He died thinking that he had not changed China. Yet he had changed the world.

Additional Thoughts:
What do you wonder? What did you discover? What do you want to discuss?

#51482—Writing is Magic, Or Is It?

Sample Jottings: "Confucius, the Great Chinese Philosopher"

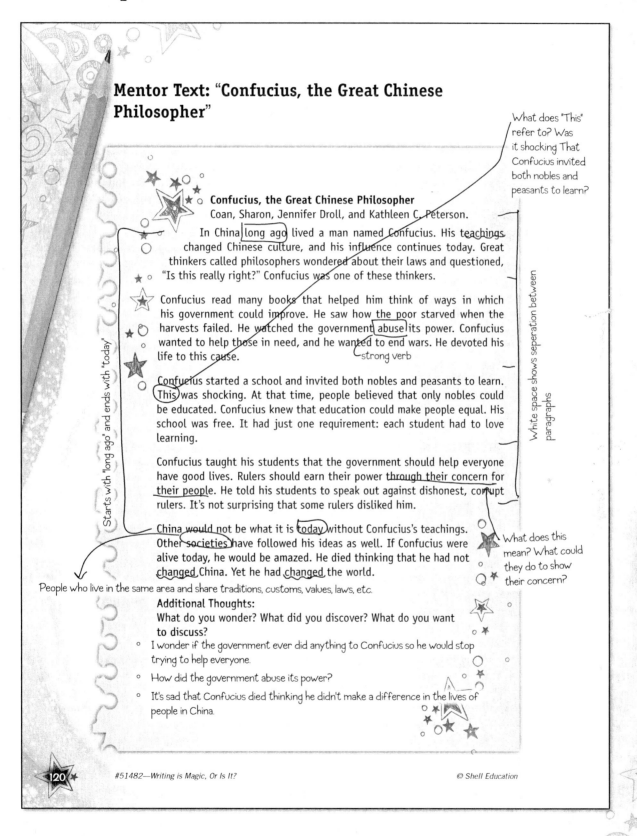

Mentor Text: "Confucius, the Great Chinese Philosopher"

What does "This" refer to? Was it shocking That Confucius invited both nobles and peasants to learn?

Confucius, the Great Chinese Philosopher
Coan, Sharon, Jennifer Droll, and Kathleen C. Peterson.

In China long ago lived a man named Confucius. His teachings changed Chinese culture, and his influence continues today. Great thinkers called philosophers wondered about their laws and questioned, "Is this really right?" Confucius was one of these thinkers.

Confucius read many books that helped him think of ways in which his government could improve. He saw how the poor starved when the harvests failed. He watched the government abuse its power. Confucius wanted to help those in need, and he wanted to end wars. He devoted his life to this cause.

strong verb

Confucius started a school and invited both nobles and peasants to learn. This was shocking. At that time, people believed that only nobles could be educated. Confucius knew that education could make people equal. His school was free. It had just one requirement: each student had to love learning.

White space shows seperation between paragraphs

Confucius taught his students that the government should help everyone have good lives. Rulers should earn their power through their concern for their people. He told his students to speak out against dishonest, corrupt rulers. It's not surprising that some rulers disliked him.

China would not be what it is today without Confucius's teachings. Other societies have followed his ideas as well. If Confucius were alive today, he would be amazed. He died thinking that he had not changed China. Yet he had changed the world.

What does this mean? What could they do to show their concern?

Starts with "long ago" and ends with "today"

People who live in the same area and share traditions, customs, values, laws, etc.

Additional Thoughts:
What do you wonder? What did you discover? What do you want to discuss?
○ I wonder if the government ever did anything to Confucius so he would stop trying to help everyone.
○ How did the government abuse its power?
○ It's sad that Confucius died thinking he didn't make a difference in the lives of people in China.

Close Reading: "Confucius, the Great Chinese Philosopher"

💬 What does the text say?

1. Have students read the excerpt independently or with you and record their "jottings" by noting language and features in it that were interesting, puzzling, or challenging. To initiate a close read, in which you help students construct and monitor comprehension, have students share their jottings and then use the following questions or those you create to dig deeply into the text.

2. Reread the first paragraph and ask, "What did the author mean when he or she wrote that Confucius' influence continues today?'" If students do not have a response, let them know that they will return to this question later in the lesson.

3. In this same paragraph, ask how the author helps readers understand what *philosophers* means.

4. Ask: How did the third paragraph build from the second paragraph? Students might notice that in the second paragraph, the author lets us know that Confucius paid attention to people around him and was interested in helping them, even if his government was not as responsive as he would have liked. In the third paragraph, the author focuses on education as one means of helping people from all classes improve their quality of their lives.

5. The author lets us know (in the third paragraph) why Confucius worked against the beliefs of his time. Ask: Why was education so important to him? (Answer: He believed education would enable everyone to be equal.)

6. Ask: What are some facts you learned from this reading? Students may note that Confucius lived long ago in China and that he was a philosopher.

7. Ask: What one word would you use to describe Confucius? What evidence do you have? Students may suggest, for instance, that he was smart; he was a great thinker; he was passionate; and he devoted his life to ending wars and helping the less fortunate.

8. Call attention to the final paragraph. Ask: What does *societies* mean in this sentence. "Other societies have followed his ideas as well?" Students may know that societies are groups of people who live in the same location and often share similar traditions, customs, beliefs, values, and laws.

> **Close reading** is "an instructional routine in which students critically examine a text, especially through repeated readings" (Fisher and Frey 2012, 179). Using a short passage, students read carefully to determine what the text says and to uncover specific instances of the author's craft, including items such as word choice, sentence structure, endings, leads, and more.

💬 How does the text say it?

Here is the part when you invite students to reveal the pigeons tucked up the magician's sleeve. The intent of this section is to talk through *how* the text says what it says and to investigate the choices the author makes to reveal meaning.

1. Begin by asking students what they noticed about the second sentence in the first paragraph. Guide them to recognize that it is composed of two small sentences that are connected with *and* (a conjunction). If students are familiar with FANBOYS (see the lesson on coordinating conjunctions earlier in this chapter), they may identify this sentence as an example of the FANBOYS convention.

2. Have students circle the first word in each paragraph. Ask: What did you notice? They should see that paragraphs 2, 3, and 4 all begin with the word *Confucius*. Next, have them box the second word in each paragraph. Ask: What did you notice? In this case, they should have boxed verbs (*read, started, taught*). Ask students why they think the author used this pattern. Since we cannot know for sure, accept any reasonable answer (e.g., to emphasize what Confucius did to make him an important historic figure, or so the details do not get lost in the narrative.)

3. Direct students' attention to paragraph three. Ask why the author used a colon in the last sentence. In chapter 4 students learned that a colon can signal a list (see Why a Colon?). In this case, the author is signaling an explanation or example. "It had just one requirement: each student had to love learning." When readers get to the colon, they may ask, *what is the one requirement?* The author provides the answer after the colon.

4. Finally, reread the last two sentences. Ask which word the author used in both sentences? (Answer: changed) Discuss why the author may have chosen to do this. Explain that it is sometimes better to use synonyms rather than repeat a word, especially if the words are used in close proximity. In this case, however, *changed* is a key word for this essay. Have students look back to the second sentence, where they will see this word *changed* used for the first time. *Change,* or Confucius's efforts to affect *change,* is at the core of the essay. Explain that in the last paragraph, the author may have repeated *changed* (or *had not changed*) for effect and to emphasize this key idea.

Zooming In: Analyzing Writing Strategies

Here are three strategies the author used. You can also implement these with your students by following the suggested lesson ideas below.

1. **White Space:** Writers can signal a new paragraph by indenting the first word or by leaving white space between paragraphs. In "Confucius," the author chose to leave white spaces, perhaps to provide readers with a slightly longer break in which to process the information in each paragraph.

2. **Fulfilling a Promise:** In this strategy, created by Muriel Harris (as cited in McAndrew and Reigstad 2001, 44), authors make a promise to write about one topic or thesis, and then they evaluate their writing to see how well they have kept their promise. In our lesson, we identify the promise the author of "Confucius" made (to talk about Confucius as a philosopher who tried to help people in China) and how the author fulfilled this promise.

3. **Word Choice—Strong Verbs:** Writers of narrative texts are probably aware of how important it is to use strong verbs. It is reasonable to expect that this holds true for informative/explanatory and narrative nonfiction, too. The author of "Confucius" uses verbs such as *starved, failed, believed, taught,* and *changed* to express beliefs and actions.

Lesson Ideas: "Confucius, the Great Chinese Philosopher"

Once you and your students have identified instances of author's craft, we believe it is important to name the strategies and to empower students to try out the strategies in their own writing. These lesson ideas provide you with opportunities for your students to practice the strategies with support from you and their peers.

White Space

1. Explain, as Lane (1993) did in *After "The End,"* that there are several times when writers want to begin new paragraphs, such as a "new idea or shift in direction," or "a shift in thought, a movement in a story, a change in point of view, or a change in speaker" (122).

2. Let students know that Barry Lane (1993), a writer and teacher of writers, thinks "a paragraph is like a giant period at the end of a clump of sentences" (123). Ask: What did he mean by this? Do you agree?

3. Look back at "Confucius." Ask: How many paragraphs are there? How do you know? Hopefully, students will notice the white spaces that separate paragraphs.

4. Ask: Why do you think the author used white space instead of indentations? Invite students to offer their thinking and explain that Barry Lane (1993) believes, "A paragraph is where the writer wants to create space in the reader's mind" (123). Discuss this statement. Perhaps white space allows readers a few extra seconds to think about the content before moving on in their reading. It is up to writers to decide whether they indent or leave spaces between paragraphs. Either way is acceptable, but it is inappropriate to use both formats in the same text.

5. Return to "Confucius" and select students to read aloud one paragraph at a time. What effect did the white spaces have on your reading and your comprehension? Students may say that the white spaces helped them visually see and group the ideas of a paragraph together or allowed them time to process the information more easily than they might have done without the white space.

6. As students read narrative fiction, informative/explanatory, and narrative nonfiction, have them notice whether authors choose to indent or use white space. Which do students prefer? Why?

Fulfilling a Promise

1. Initiate a discussion about promises. Ask what promises are and why people keep them.

2. Explain that writers make promises to readers; they promise to write about one topic throughout a text. In this strategy, writers "list the major ideas used in the draft and evaluate how well each helps the piece fulfill the promise" (Muriel Harris as cited in McAndrew and Reigstad 2001, 44).

3. Working individually, in pairs, or in small groups, have students test out the promise the author of "Confucius" made. Guide them to think about the thesis or focus of the piece. They may begin with the title and say that Confucius was a great Chinese philosopher. They may also point out that he did many things to help people improve the quality of their lives.

Next, have students highlight parts of each paragraph that fulfill this promise. Gather students together, and discuss how each piece of evidence helped "fulfill the promise." Students should be able to see that most of this essay talks about Confucius as a great philosopher and humanitarian.

Word Choice: Strong Verbs

1. Begin by reviewing verbs as a part of speech. Ask: What is a verb? According to Grammar-Monster, "Verbs are doing words. A verb can express a physical action, a mental action, or a state of being" (http://www.grammar-monster.com/lessons/verbs.htm).

2. Prepare some flashcards with verbs on them and have students sort them into the three categories mentioned above (e.g., physical action—burrowed; mental action—pondered; state of being—was).

3. Next, prepare a few sentences and have students underline the verbs (which are italicized). For example, Foxes *live* in packs. They *are* omnivorous mammals. They often *pounce* on their prey.

4. Turn everyone's attention to "Confucius." Have students, with your guidance if needed, circle the verbs (e.g., *lived, changed, continues, wondered, questioned,* and *was*).

5. Have students "rate" the effectiveness or strength of each verb by writing a number from 1 to 4 beside each verb. A "1" signifies a weak verb, while "4" signifies a strong verb. Before sending students off to work on "Confucius," try out the rating system with the following sentences. Write the sentences on a board or chart paper, have students identify the verbs (*went, searched, arrived,* and *resumed*) and rate each one from 1 to 4. Students should have a rationale for their ratings.

    a. On April 18, 1775, hundreds of British troops went from Boston to Concord.

    b. The British searched for weapons.

    c. More Mintuemen arrived in Concord.

    d. The Colonists resumed their attack.

Students may say *went* = 1, *searched* = 2, *arrived* = 2, and *resumed* = 4. The important part of this activity is not the rating the verbs receive; the important part takes place in the discussion that follows. It is during the discussion that students make visible their understandings of strong verbs and the roles they play in conveying the author's message. Note state-of-being (or linking) verbs should not be used in this activity.

Extension

Arrange students in partners. Have one student write a sentence with a weak verb and pass it to his or her partner. The partner revises with a stronger, appropriate verb. Switch roles and repeat.

Reflection Questions

1. As noted in the chapter's introduction, this genre is known by several names: *narrative nonfiction, creative nonfiction,* or *literary nonfiction.* Which one do you prefer? Why? What connotations does each name suggest?

2. Which texts from your classroom library or from materials you use for reading instruction could you classify as narrative nonfiction? How might you use these texts for writing instruction?

#51482—Writing is Magic, Or Is It?

Chapter 6

Opinion/Argument Writing

During a collaborative meeting of teachers, one first-grade teacher, Debby, explained that her student had written a letter to his family stating the claim that he should have his own bedroom. He supported his claim with reasons. For example, his brother talked to him a lot at night and that kept him from sleeping, so he thought he would get more sleep if he had his own room. After his parents agreed that he could have his own room, he invited his older brother to join him in his new bedroom! Debby then told the story of another student who had convinced her mother, through writing, to let her repaint her bedroom lavender. Not long after the letter went home, Debby received a photograph of the student with her mother, gliding paint rollers along fresh lavender walls. Whether stating a claim for a new bedroom, for a fresh paint color, or for a positive action that will make the world a better place, it is important to keep in mind that "letter writers see the world as it is, imagine what it could be, and use writing to make dreams come true" (Picard Taylor 2008, 17). There are everyday opportunities all around us that call for opinion/argument writing.

As the Common Core State Standards explain, "although young children are not able to produce fully developed logical arguments, they develop a variety of methods to extend and elaborate their work by providing examples, offering reasons for their assertions, and explaining cause and effect" (Appendix A, 23). Providing students with opportunities to communicate their opinions through writing is important, as "these kinds of expository structures are steps on the road to argument" (Appendix A, 23). In fact, the Common Core State Standards assign the term *opinion* to these types of developing arguments written by students in Kindergarten through fifth grade.

However, the use of the terms *opinion*, *persuasion*, and *argument* in the Common Core State Standards can be puzzling, and defining each term allows us to understand their differences.

Opinion writing often, "takes a stand on a topic and supports opinions with facts, definitions, and details" (writestepswriting.com 2013). However, opinion writing does not necessarily require facts to support the opinion presented. For example, opinion is also defined as "a view or judgment formed about something, not necessarily based on fact or knowledge" (Google search, "opinion"). For young children, opinion writing is about sharing their personal beliefs.

Persuasive writing, on the other hand, "focuses on convincing the reader to agree with the author" and the author, "uses logic and facts to persuade the reader" (writestepswriting.com 2013).

The term *argument* takes convincing to another level and is "used to support claims in an analysis of a topic" (WriteSteps 2013). The author "uses facts, evidence, and reasons to develop claims and opposing claims" (WriteSteps 2013). When making an argument, one supports a claim, which is similar to what lawyers do in court. They are trying to persuade, but more importantly, they are trying to present facts and evidence that *prove* that the client is innocent—or not. Both persuasion and argument can include counter arguments, examples, facts, and more.

Let us take a look at the skills and understandings identified in the English Language Arts Standards for Argument Writing (CCSS 2010). These standards reflect what students should know and be able to do by the end of the identified academic year. As you look horizontally across the rows in the following chart, you will find the skills and understandings associated with writing argument texts in grades 3–8. Looking vertically down each column, you will see how each skill or understanding increases in complexity. Rather than rewrite the standard in each box, only the changes/additions from grade to grade are included, as reflected in the language that we have taken directly from the standards.

Figure 6.1: Opinion/Argument Writing Standards Grades 3-8

Grade	Skills and Understandings Students Must Demonstrate by the End of Each Grade					
	Introduce a Topic	Develop a Topic	Link Ideas/ Transitions	Precise Language	Formal Style	Concluding Statement
Grade 3	Introduce the topic or text they are writing about, state an opinion, and create an organizational structure that lists reasons.	Provide reasons that support the opinion.	Use linking words and phrases (e.g., **because, therefore, since, for example**) to connect opinion and reasons.	N/A	N/A	Provide a concluding statement or section.
Grade 4	Introduce a topic or text clearly... related ideas are grouped to support the writer's purpose.	... supported by facts and details.	Link opinion and reasons using words and phrases (e.g., **for instance, in order to, in addition**).	N/A	N/A	... related to the opinion presented.
Grade 5	...logically grouped...	...logically ordered reasons that are supported by facts and details.	...and clauses (e.g., **consequently, specifically**).	N/A	N/A	same as Grade 4

#51482—Writing is Magic, Or Is It?

Grade	Skills and Understandings Students Must Demonstrate by the End of Each Grade *cont.*					
	Introduce a Topic	**Develop a Topic**	**Link Ideas/ Transitions**	**Precise Language**	**Formal Style**	**Concluding Statement**
Grade 6	Introduce claim(s) and organize the reasons and evidence clearly.	Support claim(s) with clear reasons and relevant evidence, using credible sources and demonstrating an understanding of the topic or text.	Use words, phrases, and clauses to clarify the relationships among claim(s) and reasons.	N/A	Establish and maintain formal style.	Provide a concluding statement or section that follows from the argument presented.
Grade 7	...acknowledge alternate or opposing claims...	...with logical reasoning and relevant evidence, using accurate, credible sources...	...to create cohesion and clarify the relationships among claim(s), reasons, and evidence.	N/A	same as Grade 6	...and supports the argument presented.
Grade 8	...distinguish the claim(s) from alternate or opposing claims, and organize the reasons and evidence logically.	...and demonstrating an understanding of the topic or text.	...counterclaims...	N/A	same as Grade 6	same as Grade 7

Writing Strategies Used in Opinion/Argument Writing

The authors of *opinion*, *persuasive*, and *argument* writing pieces in this chapter use the following writing strategies. Through close reading, we identify the following strategies, and we discuss how the writers use the strategies to communicate and enhance the meaning of their messages.

Concluding Statement—For One and All: When writers end with a concise statement that reiterates the main point of the writing piece, readers are left with a clear take-away message.

Highlight to Group Reasons and their Examples: Color can help writers group and organize related ideas in order to present a logically sequenced writing piece, providing clarity and minimizing confusion.

Words and Phrases that Speak to the Heart: When writing an opinion piece about an emotional topic, writers can use words and phrases that are full of emotion and tug at the reader's heart. This way, the reader understands the writer's opinion.

Speak Directly to Your Audience: Some believe that all opinion/argument writing should have an objective tone, but this is not the case. Speaking directly to your target audience and communicating your personality can help to create a powerfully convincing piece.

You will find a clean "student copy" of each mentor text in Appendix B. If you think your students will be able to understand, or at least get the gist of the text on their own, begin by providing them with copies of the text, have them read it independently (or with a partner), and annotate it as they read. In their jottings, they should note text features (e.g., italicized words, headings, and key words), interesting or unfamiliar use of language, the organizational structure of the text, questions the text raises for them, author's craft (e.g., alliteration, metaphor, varied sentence constructions, effective leads, transitions, and conclusions). If you think the text may be too challenging for your students to comprehend independently, distribute the clean copy and then engage in a guided close read. (See the next two sections for guidance.)

Once students have read and annotated the text (i.e., completed their "jottings"), call them together into a large group to discuss the content of the text (i.e., *What* does the text say?) and then to investigate how the author crafted the text (i.e., *How* does the text say it?). Rather than share our sample jottings directly with your students, we envision that you will use our annotations to help guide your students through the close readings.

Questioning Lead: Writers can spark interest and activate their readers' ideas about the topic of discussion by asking relevant questions at the start of the writing piece.

All Things Considered: Acknowledging and addressing viewpoints that differ from those presented can actually help to strengthen the overall claims of the piece. These alternate viewpoints can become counter arguments in which the writer discusses and refutes opposing views.

Use a Thesis Statement: Stating the claim of the argument in one concise and clear sentence helps to orient readers as they read the examples, opinions, and other support throughout the piece. Thesis statements should come in the beginning of the writing piece.

Consult a Credible Source: Facts, statistics, and information from interviews can help to provide objective support for a claim. Sources should be credible and cited within the text.

Stay Focused: It is important for writers of opinion and argument essays to stay focused on one topic throughout each text. Doing so allows the writer to develop one controlling idea and enables the reader to comprehend the writer's message.

***Who* versus *That*:** *Who* is used when writers talk about people. *That* is used when referring to an object.

Mentor Text (Opinion): "I Love my Grandpa"

I Love my Grandpa

By Dylyn Markham

"Bye, Dylyn, have a great day," said my grandpa to me. When I hear him say that every morning, I think to myself, "My life is great with my grandpa."

He is patient. A lot of the time my brother stomps on the table. Instead of screaming my grandpa asks, "Will you please get off the table"?

Most of the time my grandpa goes into stores with long lines. Instead of cutting people to get to the front, he waits patiently for his turn. Sometimes my grandpa has some trouble with his car. Instead of blaming it on someone else, he calmly fixes it. Also, he is a hard worker. Sometimes my grandpa mows the lawn and that is hard work because in the summer it is so hot. My grandpa fixes stuff when it needs fixing. A lot of times he fixed our computer, my Go Cart or some electronics.

My grandpa helps me with anything like my pitching, my wrestling moves, or my homework. Truly he has a great sense of humor. Yesterday my brother and my grandpa were playing bowling on the Wii when my grandpa said, "I am going to win," and my brother said, "In your dreams" and my grandpa started cracking up laughing. My grandpa is always telling jokes at dinner. My grandpa has a great laugh. When my grandpa laughs, I know it is him. Grandpas make life better.

Additional Thoughts:
What do you wonder? What did you discover? What do you want to discuss?

Sample Jottings: "I Love my Grandpa"

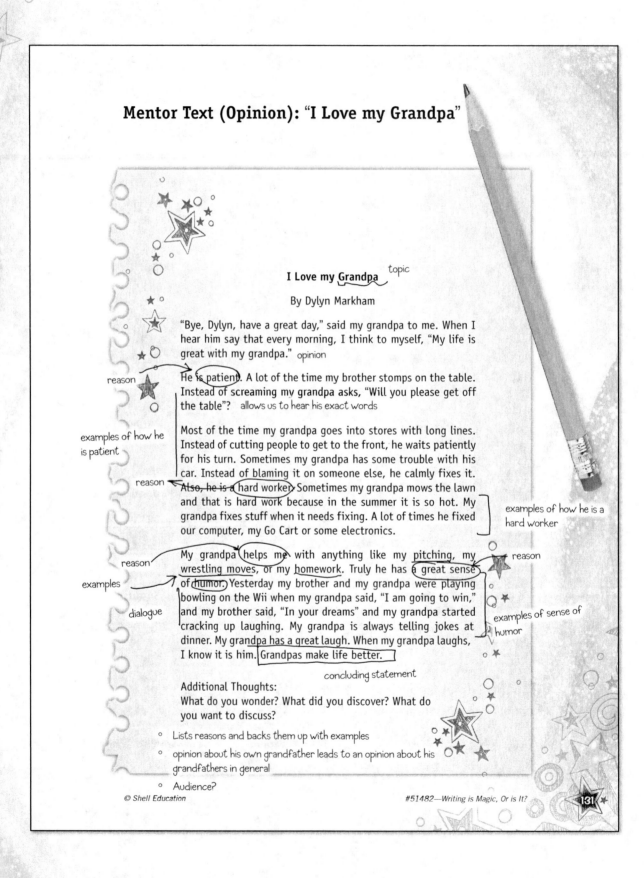

Mentor Text (Opinion): "I Love my Grandpa"

I Love my Grandpa   *topic*

By Dylyn Markham

"Bye, Dylyn, have a great day," said my grandpa to me. When I hear him say that every morning, I think to myself, "My life is great with my grandpa." *opinion*

reason → He is patient. A lot of the time my brother stomps on the table. Instead of screaming my grandpa asks, "Will you please get off the table"?   *allows us to hear his exact words*

examples of how he is patient

Most of the time my grandpa goes into stores with long lines. Instead of cutting people to get to the front, he waits patiently for his turn. Sometimes my grandpa has some trouble with his car. Instead of blaming it on someone else, he calmly fixes it.

reason → Also, he is a hard worker. Sometimes my grandpa mows the lawn and that is hard work because in the summer it is so hot. My grandpa fixes stuff when it needs fixing. A lot of times he fixed our computer, my Go Cart or some electronics.

examples of how he is a hard worker

reason   My grandpa helps me with anything like my pitching, my wrestling moves, or my homework. Truly he has a great sense of humor.   *reason*

examples   *dialogue*   Yesterday my brother and my grandpa were playing bowling on the Wii when my grandpa said, "I am going to win," and my brother said, "In your dreams" and my grandpa started cracking up laughing. My grandpa is always telling jokes at dinner. My grandpa has a great laugh. When my grandpa laughs, I know it is him. Grandpas make life better.

examples of sense of humor

concluding statement

Additional Thoughts:
What do you wonder? What did you discover? What do you want to discuss?

○ Lists reasons and backs them up with examples

○ opinion about his own grandfather leads to an opinion about his grandfathers in general

○ Audience?

© Shell Education   #51482—Writing is Magic, Or is It?   131

Close Reading: "I Love my Grandpa"

What does the text say?

The purpose of this section is to address students' comprehension and to focus on what the text says. Here, we model how to ask text-dependent questions in order to encourage students to infer meaning.

> **Close reading** is "an instructional routine in which students critically examine a text, especially through repeated readings" (Fisher and Frey 2012, 179). Using a short passage, students read carefully to determine what the text says and to uncover specific instances of the author's craft, including items such as word choice, sentence structure, endings, leads, and more.

1. Invite students to share in partnerships or small groups what they noticed about the essay. Ask: What did you jot down? What strikes you? What surprises you? Guide students in figuring out what the text is saying.

2. Begin the close reading by asking: What does the author want us to know about his grandpa? Students might respond that Dylyn wants us to know that life is great with his grandpa and the reasons why he feels this way. Discuss how the author shares his opinion about his grandpa. Guide students in locating evidence in the text.

   - Ask: What major reasons does the author list? Students will likely locate the following: he is patient; he is a hard worker; he helps him out; and he has a great sense of humor. Ask students to locate evidence for these reasons.

   - Ask: How does the author support these reasons with details? What are the specific examples he gives?

   - Ask students to find examples of how his grandpa is patient (when his brother stomps on the table, he does not scream; when he is standing in a long line, he does not cut; and he calmly fixes his car).

3. After discussing specific examples for each reason, have students locate parts of the text that allow the reader to hear his grandpa. Students will likely point out the dialogue at the beginning of the text: *"Bye, Dylyn, have a great day," said my grandpa to me* in addition to the conversation during the bowling game in which the grandpa says, *"I am going to win."* Ask: What do the grandpa's words reveal about him?

4. Ask students if there are any words in the text that are new to them. Call attention to the text, and ask students to use it to construct meanings for the following words: *Go Cart, electronics, Wii*.

   - Ask students what the author is saying when he writes the phrase *when it needs fixing* in the sentence, *My grandpa fixes stuff when it needs fixing.*

5. Have students scan the text for words and phrases that speak to their heart or call for their attention. Ask: What words or phrases are full of emotion? Students might choose the following: *When my grandpa laughs, I know it is him* or *When I hear him say that every morning, I think to myself, "My life is great with my grandpa."*

- Ask: How do these words and phrases allow you to understand and to feel the author's opinion of his grandpa? Discuss how the author uses an emotional tone to convey his opinion to his readers.

6. Point out the last line of the text: *Grandpas make life better.* Ask: Why do you think the author transitions from his opinion about his own grandpa to his opinion about grandpas in general?

7. Finally, ask students to discuss: Who is the audience for this writing piece? Who do you think the author intends to share his opinion of his grandpa with? Who does the author want to know that, *Grandpas make life better?*

How does the text say it?

Here is the part when you invite students to reveal the pigeons tucked up the magician's sleeve. The intent of this section is to talk through *how* the author uses literary devices, craft strategies, and structure to reveal meaning.

1. Begin by asking the students to reread the first paragraph of the text:

   "Bye Dylyn, have a great day," said my grandpa to me. When I hear him say that every morning, I think to myself, "My life is great with my grandpa."

2. Ask: What is the author up to when he uses dialogue right at the start of the story? Discuss how the dialogue allows us to hear his exact words and, therefore, draws us into the author's emotional opinion from the beginning.

   - Ask: What other craft strategy does the author use to do this in the first paragraph? Discuss how the author uses what is called a *thoughtshot* and allows the reader to hear exactly what he thinks.

3. Have students think about the structure of the text, specifically, how he provides a reason and then follows the reasons with specific examples. Discuss how this logical sequence allows the reader to understand how the author developed his opinion of his grandpa. Ask: How does grouping the reason with examples help you?

   In order to create a thoughtshot, writers stop the action for a brief moment and reveal what a character is thinking or feeling (Lane 1993). Thoughtshots allow the reader to hear the exact words that the character is thinking. Writers often signal the use of a thoughtshot with phrases including, *I thought to myself* or *I kept thinking* or *I said to myself* or *I wondered*. The exact thoughts are written in quotations or in italics.

4. Ask students to notice another aspect of structure, specifically how the author uses paragraphs. Discuss: Are different reasons grouped together? For example, invite students to reread the last paragraph. Discuss how this one paragraph includes two major reasons (that his grandpa helps him and that his grandpa has a great sense of humor).

   - Ask what was the author up to when he grouped these two different ideas into one paragraph? Would it be helpful to have one reason per paragraph, or does grouping reasons work for you?

- Ask students to reread the text, noticing how the other reasons are grouped.

5. Direct students to paragraph three that begins, "Most of the time..." Ask: How does the author transition from the reasons to the examples in this paragraph? Point out the words and phrases: *most of the time, sometimes, also, a lot of times.*

6. Remind students about their discussion of how the author uses words and phrases that touch the reader's heart. Ask students to notice where in the text these phrases are located (beginning and end).

- Have students discuss what the author is up to when he starts and ends with words and phrases that hold emotion. How does this draw us in as readers? How does this strategy make us feel as if we agree with the author's opinion, even though we have never met his grandpa?

Zooming In: Analyzing Writing Strategies

Here are three strategies that the author uses that you can also implement with students using the suggested lesson ideas that follow.

1. **Highlight to Group Reasons and their Examples:** The writer groups his reasons for thinking that life is great with his grandfather with specific examples. Although this writer groups different reasons in one paragraph, writers might also use paragraphing to separate the major reasons for readers. Color can help writers group and organize related ideas in order to present a logically sequenced writing piece, providing clarity and minimizing confusion.

2. **Words and Phrases that Speak to the Heart:** The writer writes his opinion about a topic that is close to his heart. He uses words and phrases that are full of emotion, tugging at the reader's heart, too. This way, the reader understands the writer's opinion. He uses these heartfelt words and phrases at the beginning and at the end of his opinion piece. For example, he writes: *When my grandpa laughs, I know it is him* or *When I hear him say that every morning, I think to myself, "My life is great with my grandpa."*

3. **Concluding Statement: For One and All:** The writer ends his opinion piece by writing the concluding statement: *Grandpas make life better.* This concise statement reiterates the main point of the writing piece, and we are left with a clear take-away message.

Lesson Ideas: "I Love my Grandpa"

Once you and your students have identified instances of author's craft, we believe it is important to name the strategies and to empower students to try out the strategies in their own writing. These lesson ideas provide you with opportunities for your students to practice the strategies with support from you and their peers.

Group Reasons and their Examples

Teach students that color can help them organize the structure of their opinion piece by grouping reasons and examples.

1. Have available highlighters of four different colors. Using the text "I Love my Grandpa," choose one color and guide students in highlighting each reason with its related examples all in that color to show their relationship. As you and the students highlight, complete the following chart:

Overall Opinion	Reason	Examples to Support Reason
Life is great with my grandpa.	patient	He does not scream at his brother when his brother is on the table; he does not cut the long line, he calmly fixes his car.
Same	hard worker	He mows the lawn; he fixes stuff including the computer, Go Cart, and electronics.
Same	helps the author	Helps with pitching, wrestling moves, and homework.
Same	great sense of humor	Laughing and joking during Wii game and telling jokes

2. Once the related reasons and examples are highlighted, have students cut out the groups. Model how to play with the paragraph arrangement, making one paragraph per reason. Discuss: Is it helpful to have each reason and the related examples in its own paragraph? Why?

3. Invite students to highlight related reasons and examples in their own opinion pieces. Have them share their findings and how they might want to revise the grouping or paragraphing of their drafts and why.

Extension

Have students experiment with the use of specific linking words to connect the overall opinion (life is great with his grandpa) to the reasons. Together with the class, brainstorm such words and phrases, including *because, therefore, since, for example, for instance, in addition* (CCSS). Guide students in flagging places in the text in which a linking word would be helpful to the reader. Reread the writing piece with the linking words and discuss: How do the linking words affect the flow of the ideas for the reader?

Words and Phrases that Speak to the Heart

Teach students that, when writing an opinion piece about a topic that is close to their heart, they can use heartfelt words and phrases in order to draw in the reader and encourage the reader to understand their opinion. When readers *feel*, they understand.

1. Remove the heartfelt words and phrases from the text "I Love my Grandpa." Reread the text without the heartfelt words, and have students discuss the effect of their absence.

2. Gather texts appropriate for your grade level that contain words and phrases that speak to the heart. These texts might be opinion pieces, but they could also be poems, letters, greeting cards, obituaries, tributes, messages written on napkins, and narratives.

3. Have the students locate words and phrases from the collection that tug at their hearts and ask them to keep a running list.

4. Invite students to choose one of the words or phrases they found. Using a digital recording device that is available to you, record each student saying the word or phrase they found that speaks to their heart.

5. Compile the recordings, and play them in sequence. Ask students to discuss the emotional tone of the messages.

6. Send students to their writers' notebooks. Have them list a topic for an opinion piece that is meaningful to them. This might be how they feel about a family member or an environmental issue. Ask them to jot a list of related words and phrases that could be used in an opinion piece about the topic.

Concluding Statement: For One and All

1. Display the following concluding statement from the text, "I Love my Granapa": "Grandpas make life better." Have students discuss what makes this a concluding statement, and brainstorm some alternate statements that could also be used for this writing piece. Students might brainstorm idea such as the following: I cannot imagine a world without grandpas, or Grandpas make the world a better place.

2. Gather a collection of opinion pieces. Provide students with a variety of subjects and types, including movie, book, restaurant, and vacation reviews.

3. Have students work in groups, reading a collection of opinion pieces and locating the concluding sentence of each one. Ask students to add the concluding statement to an ongoing chart entitled "Concluding Statements in Opinion Writing." When a writing piece lacks a concluding statement, invite students to write one and add it to the chart.

4. Ask students to revisit their own opinion pieces and try out the strategy of adding a concluding statement.

Mentor Text (Persuasive): "Dear Mr. and Mrs. Chase"

Dear Mr. and Mrs. Chase,

Have you been feeling Trevor is bored with his daily life? Have you found yourself wanting to shake things up a bit at home? I, myself, think that your son, Trevor Chase, should be able to get a lizard. Yes, lizards are unique pets but they are easily contained and could help teach Trevor some more responsibility, not that he already isn't responsible.

The lizard will teach Trevor responsibility by letting him clean its cage and holding it with care. Trevor will become a smarter kid with the learning the lizard will give him. The lizard will be medium level care, so he won't have to take care of the lizard 24/7 and he will still have time to play all the sports he does. Trevor will still need to do the basic care though. If he could play with a lizard, he wouldn't be bugging you all the time. If Trevor could get a lizard, he would be playing less video games and spending more time with his lizard and his friends. This would be a great choice for everyone. This might be a bad idea because he may want to experiment with his lizard. I understand that your family has a dog, so just make sure none of Trevor's friends try to feed the dog.

Maybe Trevor is having a hard time focusing on homework because all that is going through his mind is that lizard. Maybe he will be able to focus knowing there is a lizard named Stevie waiting in his room. There is also a downside to that. He would always be wanting to see his lizard. He will learn that Stevie will not be going anywhere and the lizard will still be there when Trevor goes to see him. Trevor can also have an educational experience from learning about lizards. Trevor could do many reports on lizards and even give the audience a little treat about the report.

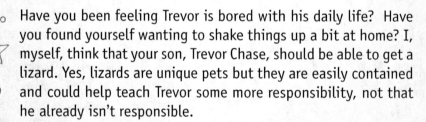

 #51482—Writing is Magic, Or Is It?

I believe that lizards are easy to maintain. They need care and the right temperature to survive. Lizards are pretty tough animals so they do not need your care all of the time. I think Trevor will be able to feed Stevie once a day, and he also will have to work hard for money for a nice cage and lamp so his cage will be just like in the wild. Trevor will need to clean the cage about every week or so to keep Stevie and Trevor happy. The downside to this is that since Trevor plays many sports, he might not have the time to clean the cage every week but I believe that he will be just fine.

Trevor is a good kid as I have heard, but maybe a lizard will make him even better. Even though it may be a little extra work, I personally think it is worth it. I personally have a Komodo Dragon, which is one of the biggest lizards on the planet. Even a lizard that big isn't that hard to take care of. The last thing I have to say is that Trevor will be happy with his new friend, Stevie. I hope this will convince you!

Thank you for reading.

Yours truly,

Trevor

Additional Thoughts:
What do you wonder? What did you discover? What do you want to discuss?

Sample Jottings: "Dear Mr. and Mrs. Chase"

Mentor Text (Persuasive): "Dear Mr. and Mrs. Chase"

Dear Mr. and Mrs. Chase, — *writes directly to a specific audience*

lead: questioning — Have you been feeling Trevor is bored with his daily life? Have you found yourself wanting to shake things up a bit at home? I, myself, think that your son, Trevor Chase, should be able to get a lizard. — *clearly states claim* — Yes, lizards are unique pets but they are easily contained and could help teach Trevor some more responsibility, not that he already isn't responsible. — *informal tone/ shows voice*

The lizard will teach Trevor responsibility by letting him clean its cage and holding it with care. Trevor will become a smarter kid with the learning the lizard will give him. The lizard will be medium level care, so he won't have to take care of the lizard 24/7 and he will still have time to play all the sports he does. Trevor will still need to do the basic care though. If he could play with a lizard, he wouldn't be bugging you all the time. If Trevor could get a lizard, he would be playing less video games and spending more time with his lizard and his friends. This would be a great choice for everyone. This might be a bad idea because he may want to experiment with his lizard. I understand that your family has a dog, so just make sure none of Trevor's friends try to feed the dog. — *specific reasons to support the claim*

"If" shows relationship between claim and reasons

links ideas

considers "why not" to get a lizard — Maybe Trevor is having a hard time focusing on homework because all that is going through his mind is that lizard. Maybe he will be able to focus knowing there is a lizard named Stevie waiting in his room. There is also a downside to that. He would always be wanting to see his lizard. He will learn that Stevie will not be going anywhere and the lizard will still be there when Trevor goes to see him. Trevor can also have an educational experience from learning about lizards. Trevor could do many reports on lizards and even give the audience a little treat about the report. — *"downside" addressed*

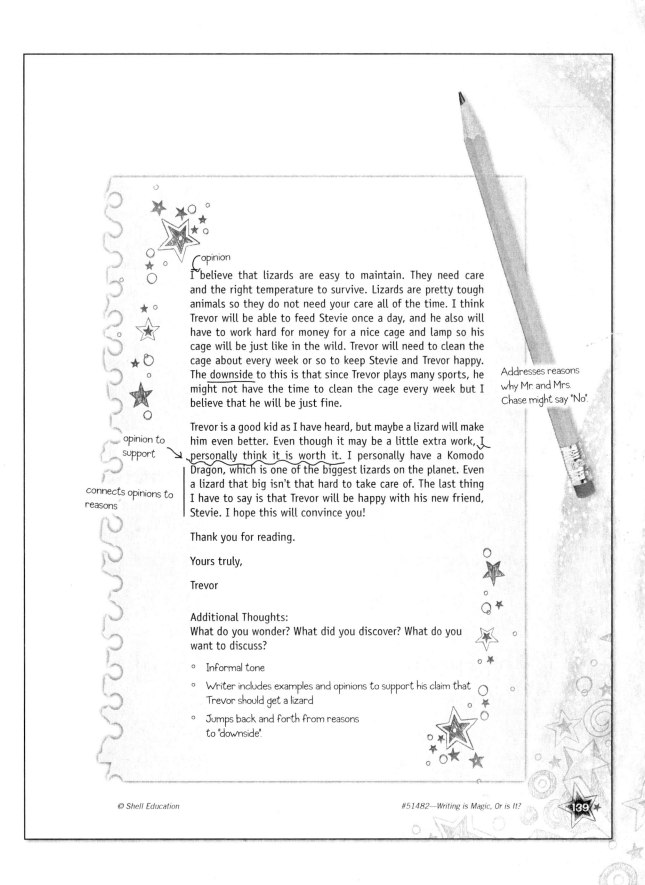

opinion

I believe that lizards are easy to maintain. They need care and the right temperature to survive. Lizards are pretty tough animals so they do not need your care all of the time. I think Trevor will be able to feed Stevie once a day, and he also will have to work hard for money for a nice cage and lamp so his cage will be just like in the wild. Trevor will need to clean the cage about every week or so to keep Stevie and Trevor happy. The downside to this is that since Trevor plays many sports, he might not have the time to clean the cage every week but I believe that he will be just fine.

Addresses reasons why Mr. and Mrs. Chase might say "No".

opinion to support

connects opinions to reasons

Trevor is a good kid as I have heard, but maybe a lizard will make him even better. Even though it may be a little extra work, I personally think it is worth it. I personally have a Komodo Dragon, which is one of the biggest lizards on the planet. Even a lizard that big isn't that hard to take care of. The last thing I have to say is that Trevor will be happy with his new friend, Stevie. I hope this will convince you!

Thank you for reading.

Yours truly,

Trevor

Additional Thoughts:
What do you wonder? What did you discover? What do you want to discuss?

○ Informal tone

○ Writer includes examples and opinions to support his claim that Trevor should get a lizard

○ Jumps back and forth from reasons to "downside".

Close Reading: "Dear Mr. and Mrs. Chase"

💬 What does the text say?

The purpose of this section is to address students' comprehension and to focus on what the text says. Here, we model how to ask text-dependent questions in order to encourage students to infer meaning.

> **Close reading** is "an instructional routine in which students critically examine a text, especially through repeated readings" (Fisher and Frey 2012, 179). Using a short passage, students read carefully to determine what the text says and to uncover specific instances of the author's craft, including items such as word choice, sentence structure, endings, leads, and more.

1. Invite students to share in partnerships what they noticed about the writing piece. Ask: What did you jot down? What strikes you? What surprises you? Guide students in figuring out what the text is saying.

2. Begin the close reading by asking: To whom is the author speaking to? Discuss how the author is speaking directly to Mr. and Mrs. Chase. Ask: Who are Mr. and Mrs. Chase? Have students locate evidence in the text that allows the reader to infer that Mr. and Mrs. Chase are Trevor's parents. Ask students who they think the author might be. Is the author Trevor's friend? Could the author be Trevor himself? Is the author writing in the third person? Invite students to support their opinion by finding examples that allow them to infer.

3. Ask students what type of writing the author chose to write (a personal letter). Ask: How do you know? Students should point to the greeting and to the closing of the letter.

4. Discuss: What is the author's purpose in writing a letter to Mr. and Mrs. Chase? After students point out that the author is trying to convince Mr. and Mrs. Chase to let Trevor have a lizard, ask them to reread the first paragraph and locate the clearly stated claim.

5. Point out the word *downside* and have students explain or infer what the word means, using context clues to support their thinking. Ask: Do you want to clarify the meaning of any other words in the text? Students might ask about a *Komodo Dragon*.

6. Have students name the major reasons the author uses to try to convince Mr. and Mrs. Chase to let Trevor get a lizard. Ask students to locate the evidence in the text.

7. Ask students to locate places in the text in which the author discusses a *downside*. Ask: What does the author say about the downside?

8. Finally, ask students to describe the overall tone of the letter. Is it serious? Humorous? What is the narrator's personality? Have them locate examples to support their thoughts. Students will likely share that the letter is light-hearted or funny ("If he could play with a lizard, he wouldn't be bugging you all the time"). They will probably find the narrator's personality to be easy-going or

fun-loving ("I understand that your family has a dog, so just make sure none of Trevor's friends try to feed the dog").

How does the text say it?

Here is the part when you invite students to reveal the pigeons tucked up the magician's sleeve. The intent of this section is to talk through *how* the author uses literary devices, craft strategies, and structure to reveal meaning.

1. Begin by asking: What exactly does the author do to create the informal tone of the letter? Direct students to phrases such as *not that he isn't responsible*, or *Maybe Trevor is having a hard time focusing* or *so just make sure none of Trevor's friends*.

2. Have students reread the following: *I understand that your family has a dog...* Discuss how the author uses the strategy of speaking directly to Mr. and Mrs. Chase. Ask: How does the author's choice to speak directly to the audience and to include personal details affect the message?

3. Ask: What words or phrases does the author use to create humor? Discuss the following phrase: *Trevor is a good kid as I have heard...* Ask: What is the author up to here?

4. Invite students to consider the organizational structure of the letter. Talk about how the author moves back and forth between reasons and what he calls the *downside* of some of the points. Ask: How does this help to create the tone? Discuss how this structure mirrors a conversation. Invite students to share their thoughts about why the author would include a *downside*.

5. Direct students to the following sentence: *Maybe he will be able to focus knowing there is a lizard named Stevie waiting in his room.* Ask students what they think the author was doing when he includes the name of the lizard.

6. Finally, bring students back to the beginning of the letter. Ask students to consider why the author starts the letter with two questions. Discuss how he follows the questions with his opinion that Trevor should get a lizard. Talk about how this draws the reader into the writing.

Zooming In: Analyzing Writing Strategies

Here are three strategies that the author uses that you can also implement with students using the suggested lesson ideas that follow.

1. **Speak Directly to Your Audience:** The author speaks directly to Mr. and Mrs. Chase in an informal tone that is full of voice and personality. Speaking directly to your target audience and communicating your personality can help to create a powerfully convincing piece.

2. **Questioning Lead:** The author sparks interest and engages the reader right from the start by asking: *Have you been feeling Trevor is bored with his daily life? Have*

you found yourself wanting to shake things up a bit? Writers can spark interest and activate their readers' ideas about the topic of discussion by asking relevant questions at the start of the writing piece.

3. **All Things Considered:** When presenting reasons for convincing Mr. and Mrs. Chase to allow Trevor to have a lizard, the author also presents what he calls the *downside* to some of the reasons. For example, when discussing how the lizard will teach responsibility, the author writes, "the downside to this is that since Trevor plays many sports, he might not have the time to clean the cage every week...."

Lesson Ideas: "Mr. and Mrs. Chase"

Once you and your students have identified instances of author's craft, we believe it is important to name the strategies and to empower students to try out the strategies in their own writing. These lesson ideas provide you with opportunities for your students to practice the strategies with support from you and their peers.

Speak Directly to Your Audience

1. Have students lift key words, phrases, and sentences that provide evidence that the author of "Dear Mr. and Mrs. Chase" is speaking directly to a specific audience.

2. Invite students to work in partnerships, taking turns playing the role of narrator and target audience.

When taking on the *task of trying to convince a specific audience,* students often find it helpful to enlist a partner who will play the role of the target audience for them. This way, the writer has the opportunity to shape and reshape their message, by orally telling and retelling it before writing it down. Telling a message orally, which some refer to as "writing in the air," is one way to teach the strategy of speaking directly to your audience.

3. Ask the partners who are playing the role of the target audience to listen for key words, phrases, or sentences that make them feel as if they are being spoken to directly.

4. Tell students that each time they practice telling their letter aloud the words they use will change. Each version will be different.

5. Invite students to draft their letter, paying particular attention to the use of words and phrases that speak to the audience.

Extension

The author writes the letter piece in the third-person point of view, causing readers to wonder if the author is Trevor's friend or Trevor himself. This strategy adds humor and voice. Challenge students to revise their own persuasive piece by changing the point of view to the third person. Discuss: How does the third-person point of view add humor and voice?

Questioning Lead

Most likely, your students have come across the strategy of leading readers into a writing piece by asking questions. However, they might find that not all question leads seem effective. Teach your students how to write an engaging question lead that will draw readers into writing.

1. Discuss: What makes the questions effective at the beginning of "Dear Mr. and Mrs. Chase?"

2. Locate mentor texts that begin with engaging questions as the lead. Share the leads with students, and begin a chart of examples and non-examples of what to do when writing a questioning lead. For example, students might decide how many questions are too many, how vague or specific the question should be, use humor in the question, or write something about the relevance to the topic.

3. Using a mentor text they have not seen yet, cover up the questioning lead. Read the text to the students, and have them write an original questioning lead for the text.

4. Compare and contrast their questions with those of the author, and ask students to share their opinions about their favorite question and why.

All Things Considered

Teach students that writers actually strengthen their persuasive writing pieces by including opposing points or reasons, providing what the author of "Dear Mr. and Mrs. Chase" calls the *downside*. This shows readers that the author has considered different perspectives in forming his or her opinion.

1. Have students set up a three-column chart in their notebooks with the following headings: *Reasons to Get a Lizard*, *Downsides*, and *Don't Worry About the Downside Because....*

2. Encourage students to mine the text, "Dear Mr. and Mrs. Chase," for examples that fit in the preceding chart. Ask students to list the examples in the appropriate columns.

3. Invite students to participate in a debate, using their lists to help them. Add additional points as they think of them on the spot. You might choose to do this in partnerships with one partner representing the *pro* lizard side and the other partner representing the *con*. You might also decide to separate your class in half and invite them to debate as teams.

4. After the debate, debrief: What was the effect of hearing the *downside*? How is it important to address the *downside*?

5. Invite students to include opposing views in their own persuasive letters.

Suggest that they interview at least one person to research what some downsides might be. Explain that this is important because when one has a strong opinion, it is not always easy to think of downsides.

#51482—Writing is Magic, Or Is It?

Mentor Text Excerpt (Argument): "Homework Should be Banned in all Schools"

(see Appendix B for the complete text)

Homework Should be Banned in all Schools

By Alayna Melino

A 2004 study by the University of Michigan says that homework time is up 51% since 1981. Some 13 year olds are spending over 2 hours a night on homework. Students in grades 3-6 spend around 30-60 minutes a night. High schoolers spend on average 30 minutes per class, which sometimes adds up to 3.5 hours (DeNisco). According to the guidelines by the National Education Association, a student shouldn't spend more than 10 minutes per grade level per night. That means that 7th graders should only be spending 70 minutes but that's often doubled or even tripled (Morin). In Finland students receive no homework and their high school graduate rate is 93% compared to the US, which is 75% (Biljalk). Homework should be banned in all schools.

Students who receive lots of homework are the ones who usually get the most stressed out. Many kids break down emotionally, physically, and mentally under stress and most of it is coming from their schoolwork. They cry, get sick, and sometimes even puke on their test books. A 2007 American Academy of Pediatrics report claims that too much work for children and too little play could backfire down the road (Kam). Also, colleges are seeing lots of students who are showing signs of depression, perfectionism, and stress. Lee Bartel, a professor at the University of Toronto, did a study on the effects of homework and how it causes anxiety and stress. He took data from over 20,000 kids and the results showed that homework causes much stress and leads to many breakdowns and therefore it is just useless (Kam). It is only doing harm to the students and is even causing parents to stress out too. Homework is stress and anxiety that students do not need.

Additional Thoughts:
What do you wonder? What did you discover? What do you want to discuss?

Sample Jottings: "Homework Should be Banned in all Schools"

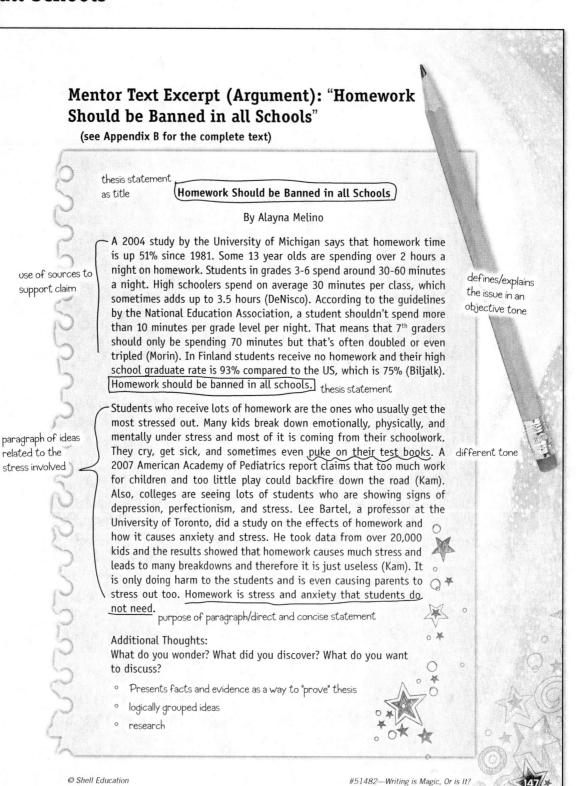

Mentor Text Excerpt (Argument): "Homework Should be Banned in all Schools"
(see Appendix B for the complete text)

thesis statement
as title

> **Homework Should be Banned in all Schools**

By Alayna Melino

use of sources to support claim

A 2004 study by the University of Michigan says that homework time is up 51% since 1981. Some 13 year olds are spending over 2 hours a night on homework. Students in grades 3-6 spend around 30-60 minutes a night. High schoolers spend on average 30 minutes per class, which sometimes adds up to 3.5 hours (DeNisco). According to the guidelines by the National Education Association, a student shouldn't spend more than 10 minutes per grade level per night. That means that 7th graders should only be spending 70 minutes but that's often doubled or even tripled (Morin). In Finland students receive no homework and their high school graduate rate is 93% compared to the US, which is 75% (Biljalk). Homework should be banned in all schools. — *thesis statement*

defines/explains the issue in an objective tone

paragraph of ideas related to the stress involved

Students who receive lots of homework are the ones who usually get the most stressed out. Many kids break down emotionally, physically, and mentally under stress and most of it is coming from their schoolwork. They cry, get sick, and sometimes even puke on their test books. A 2007 American Academy of Pediatrics report claims that too much work for children and too little play could backfire down the road (Kam). Also, colleges are seeing lots of students who are showing signs of depression, perfectionism, and stress. Lee Bartel, a professor at the University of Toronto, did a study on the effects of homework and how it causes anxiety and stress. He took data from over 20,000 kids and the results showed that homework causes much stress and leads to many breakdowns and therefore it is just useless (Kam). It is only doing harm to the students and is even causing parents to stress out too. Homework is stress and anxiety that students do not need. — *purpose of paragraph/direct and concise statement*

different tone

Additional Thoughts:
What do you wonder? What did you discover? What do you want to discuss?

- Presents facts and evidence as a way to "prove" thesis
- logically grouped ideas
- research

Close Reading: "Homework Should be Banned in all Schools"

What does the text say?

The purpose of this section is to address students' comprehension and to focus on what the text says. Here, we model how to ask text-dependent questions in order to encourage students to infer meaning.

> **Close reading** is "an instructional routine in which students critically examine a text, especially through repeated readings" (Fisher and Frey 2012, 179). Using a short passage, students read carefully to determine what the text says and to uncover specific instances of the author's craft, including items such as word choice, sentence structure, endings, leads, and more.

1. Invite students to share in small groups what they noticed about the argument. Ask: What did you jot down? What strikes you? What surprises you? Guide students in figuring out what the text is saying.

2. Begin the close reading by asking: What is the most important point in the first paragraph? How do you know? Direct the students to the thesis statement: *Homework should be banned in all schools.* Ask: What is the meaning of the word *banned*? Have students use synonyms for banned, such as *abolished*, *stopped*, or *ended*.

3. What facts did you learn in the first paragraph? What is a *study*? Ask: Which country does the author compare to the United States? Why?

4. Have students locate evidence in the text to answer the following: How much time are students spending on homework, and how much time should they spend on homework?

5. Ask students what they notice about the use of parentheses in the first paragraph. Discuss how the author includes the names of the researchers. Ask: What other sources does the author give credit to, or cite, in the first paragraph?

6. Direct students to the second paragraph and ask: What is the author's major point in the second paragraph? How do you know? Students will find that the author wants us to know that homework causes stress. Discuss with students the supporting details that allow the reader to learn about the stress and anxiety associated with homework; for example, the students *break down emotionally* and they *cry* and *get sick*.

7. Ask students to name the sources we learn from in the second paragraph. They will find the American Academy of Pediatrics and Lee Bartel (professor at the University of Toronto).

8. Discuss the meaning of the following words: *depression*, *perfectionism*, *anxiety*. Also, be sure students understand the meaning of the word *backfire*.

How does the text say it?

Here is the part when you invite students to reveal the pigeons tucked up the magician's sleeve. The intent of this section is to talk through *how* the author uses literary devices, craft strategies, and structure to reveal meaning.

1. Invite students to read the text aloud, listening for the tone of the writing. Talk about the objective, formal tone of the piece. Ask: Why do you think the author uses this tone? How does the tone communicate the message? Ask: Is there a place in which the tone changes? Students might notice the following phrase: *sometimes even puke on their test books.*

2. Have students consider how the author organizes the structure of the piece. Discuss how each paragraph contains a key sentence that sums up the point of the paragraph in addition to supporting details. Ask students to consider what the author was up to when she wrote a short, to-the-point thesis statement: *Homework should be banned in all schools.* Ask: Why would the author decide to keep this key sentence short and direct?

3. Ask: What did the author decide to use for supporting details? Discuss the power of the facts and statistics. Have students consider why the author included the researchers and organizations that helped her learn about the topic. Discuss how this strategy of including credible sources gives power to her argument.

4. Conclude by asking: Did Alayna present a convincing point of view? Have students explain their answers by identifying specific features in the writing that helped her accomplish her goals.

Zooming In: Analyzing Writing Strategies

Here are four strategies that the author uses that you can also implement with students using the suggested lesson ideas that follow.

1. **Use a Thesis Statement:** Stating the claim of the argument in one concise and clear sentence helps to orient readers as they read the examples, opinions, and other support throughout the piece. Thesis statements should come in the beginning of the writing piece.

2. **Consult a Credible Source:** Facts, statistics, and information from interviews can help to provide objective support for a claim. Sources should be credible and cited within the text.

3. **Stay Focused:** It is important for writers of opinion and argument essays to stay focused on one topic throughout each text. Doing so allows the writer to develop one controlling idea and enables the reader to comprehend the writer's message.

4. ***Who* versus *That*:** *Who* is used when writers talk about people. *That* is used when referring to an object.

Lesson Ideas: "Homework Should be Banned in all Schools"

Once you and your students have identified instances of author's craft, we believe it is important to name the strategies and to empower students to try out the strategies in their own writing. These lesson ideas provide you with opportunities for your students to practice the strategies with support from you and their peers.

Use a Thesis Statement

1. Provide students with websites that are appropriate for your grade level and contain information and examples about thesis statements. Have students research answers to the following questions: Is there more than one type of thesis statement? What is the purpose of a thesis statement?

2. Display the thesis statement from the text "Homework Should be Banned in all Schools." Discuss how the statement is right-to-the-point, concise, and direct.

3. Create and provide students with wordy thesis statements that contain unnecessary words, such as:

   • I really think that people should adopt and care for shelter dogs and that they should also foster dogs when they can.

   • It is very important to exercise each and every day, even if you do not want to exercise that much.

   • I would say that Sanibel Island is the best place to look for all kinds of different shells with your friends.

⭐ Extension

Challenge students to work in small groups to rewrite the wordy statements so that they only include words that are absolutely necessary to the meaning.

4. Make use of multimodal texts, such as videos, podcasts, and commercials. After viewing or listening to the texts, have students write a thesis statement for the message that is communicated.

A **thesis** is a statement that an author wants to prove.

Consult a Credible Source

With students, read the complete writing piece, "Homework Should be Banned in all Schools," which is located at the end of Appendix D.

1. Direct students to the reference section which lists the website of each source the author uses in the paper.

2. Tell students that they are going to investigate the sources and determine whether they think the sources are credible. Discuss the meaning of *credible*.

3. Present the following chart. Have students work in partnerships to read one of the articles online, completing the chart in order to analyze each source.

Name of the Article	What's the source?	Do you think the source is credible? Why or why not?	What information (fact, statistic, key words) does the writer of "Homework Should Be Banned in all Schools" use from the article?

4. Have each group locate the information in the article that was used by the author of "Homework Should Be Banned in all Schools." Ask: Does the author quote the exact words? Does she paraphrase? How does she cite the information within her text?

5. Provide students with an argument piece that does not include the use of information from an outside source, such as the following about the advantages of adopting a pet: http://www.thewritesource.com/studentmodels/we-adptpet.htm. Provide students with the research tools to locate a related article and add at least one piece of information from the credible source.

6. Have students reflect: How does including information from a credible source strengthen your claim?

#51482—Writing is Magic, Or Is It?

✷Extension

Locate an additional argument piece that includes sources, such as the following piece in which the author argues against a year-round school schedule:

http://www.thewritesource.com/studentmodels/ws2k-summer.htm

Invite students to add one additional source and weave it into the writing piece.

Stay Focused

It is important for writers of opinion and argument essays to stay focused on one topic throughout each text. Doing so allows the writer to develop one controlling idea and enables the reader to comprehend the writer's message.

1. Display a copy of "Homework Should Be Banned in All Schools," and have student pairs reread each sentence, keeping an eye on which sentences in the essay focus specifically on the thesis. They should discover that every sentence in the essay is used to develop the writer's controlling idea.

2. Select a piece of argument writing in which the author includes information that does not directly relate to the main point of the essay or take a look at "Zoo Field Trip" (CCSS Appendix C, 25). Identify the initial controlling idea of the essay you selected (In "Zoo Field Trip," for instance, the main point is the need to travel to a zoo to learn about conservation and wildlife preservation) and where the text strays from this focus. Discuss how a shift in focus may confuse the reader and what impact it has on the author's ability to convince his or her reader.

3. Using the same text you used in step 2 of this lesson, have students revise the essay by developing the initial controlling idea. If you used "Zoo Field Trip," for instance, your students would elaborate on what the writers of the essay could learn if allowed to take a trip to the zoo.

4. Have students share their revisions and talk about the types of evidence they included.

5. Discuss the challenges students faced, if any, when they tried to remain focused on one dominant idea across several sentences.

Who versus That

1. Provide students with a list of sentences in which the words *who* refers to people and *that* refers to an object or objects. Without explaining the targeted grammar convention, see if students can discover (or confirm) it. Use sentences you create or select from the following:

Grammar Convention: *Who* is used when writers talk about people. *That* is used when referring to an object.

- The doctor who examined the little boy gave the boy a sticker at the end of the visit.

- Airlines often charge a fee for luggage that weighs over 50 pounds.

- Players who did not attend the mandatory pre-game meeting were not allowed to play in Saturday's game.

- My grandmother asked me to water the plant that she bought at the grocery store.

- The bear that was seen wandering around the neighborhood weighs about 200 pounds.

- Sam, who owns the arcade, bought a game that will challenge even the best players.

2. Discuss the targeted grammar generalization to make sure everyone understands it. Then, using some prepared sentences, have students practice the generalization. Engage in a Thumbs Up/Thumbs Down activity. Have students use Thumbs Up when *who* should be used in the sentence and Thumbs Down when *that* should be used.

3. Next, return to "Homework Should Be Banned in All Schools" and have students reread the second paragraph, highlighting the word *who* every time it appears. Ask: Did Alayna follow the convention we are working on today? To whom does *who* refer?

4. Give students sticky notes or highlighters and challenge them to find examples of the generalization in the texts they are reading. Alternately, pass out pages from newspapers/magazines and give students 5–10 minutes to circle examples they find.

5. Have students share examples they find and determine whether each writer followed the targeted generalization.

Reflection Questions

1. What commonalities exist among *opinion*, *persuasive*, and *argument* writing? Conversely, what are some of the distinguishing characteristics of each genre?

2. What cognitive demands might your students face when creating texts in each genre? What supports can you provide to adjust for the complexities of writing in these genres?

3. Each of the three authors introduced in this chapter—Dylyn, Trevor, and Alayna—began with a different audience and purpose in mind. For what audiences and purposes could your students write opinion, persuasive, and argument pieces?

References

Anderson, Jeff. 2005. *Mechanically Inclined: Building Grammar, Usage, and Style Into Writer's Workshop*. Portland, ME: Stenhouse.

Bang, Molly, and Penny Chisholm. 2009. *Living Sunlight: How Plants Bring The Earth To Life*. New York, NY: The Blue Sky Press.

Beal, Carole R. 1996. "The Role of Comprehension Monitoring in Children's Revision." *Educational Psychology Review* 8 (3): 219–238.

Burns, Loree Griffen. 2010. *Tracking Trash: Flotsam, Jetsam and the Science of Ocean Motion*. New York, NY: HMH Books for Young Readers.

Butler, Jodie A., and M. Anne Britt. 2011. "Investigating Instruction for Improving Revision of Argumentative Essays." *Written Composition* 28 (1): 70–96.

Calkins, Lucy, Mary Ehrenworth, and Christopher Lehman. 2012. *Pathways to the Common Core: Accelerating Achievement*. Portsmouth, NH: Heinemann.

DePalma, Mary Newell. 2005. *A Grand Old Tree*. New York, NY: Arthur A. Levine Books.

Fletcher, Ralph, and JoAnn Portalupi. 2007. *Craft Lessons: Teaching Writing K–8*, 2nd ed. Portland, ME: Stenhouse Publishers.

Fisher, Douglas, and Nancy Frey. 2012. "Close Reading in Elementary Schools." *The Reading Teacher* 66: 179–188.

Flower, Linda, and John R. Hayes. 1981. "A Cognitive Process Theory of Writing." *College Composition and Communication* 32 (4): 365–387.

Flower, Linda, John R. Hayes, Linda Carey, Karen Schriver, and James Stratman. 1986. "Detection, Diagnosis, and the Strategies of Revision." *College Composition and Communication* 37 (1): 16–55.

Frost, Helen. 2008. *Monarch and Milkweed*. New York, NY: Atheneum Books for Young Readers.

Garrigues, Lisa. 2004. "Reading the Writer's Craft: The Hemingway Short Stories." *English Journal* 94 (1): 59–65.

Graham, Steve, and Dolores Perin. 2007. *Writing Next: Effective Strategies To Improve Writing Of Adolescents In Middle And High Schools—A Report To Carnegie Corporation of New York*. Washington, D.C.: Alliance for Excellent Education.

Gutkind, Lee. 2012. "What is Creative Nonfiction?" *Creative Nonfiction: True Stories, Told Well*. https://www.creativenonfiction.org/what-is-creative-nonfiction.

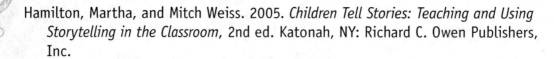

Appendix A

Hamilton, Martha, and Mitch Weiss. 2005. *Children Tell Stories: Teaching and Using Storytelling in the Classroom*, 2nd ed. Katonah, NY: Richard C. Owen Publishers, Inc.

Heard, Georgia. 1999. *Awakening the Heart*. Portsmouth, NH: Heinemann.

Lane, Barry. 1993. *After "The End": Teaching and Learning Creative Revision*. Portsmouth, NH: Heinemann.

Library of Congress. 2014. "Vermont Maple Syrup." Accessed October 10. http://www.americaslibrary.gov/es/vt/es_vt_syrup_1.html.

Lin, Shin-Ju Cindy, Brandon W. Monroe, and Gary A. Troia. 2007. "Development of Writing Knowledge in Grades 2–8: A Comparison of Typically Developing Writers and Their Struggling Peers." *Reading & Writing Quarterly: Overcoming Learning Difficulties* 23 (3): 207–230.

Lyon, George Ella. 2011. *All The Water In The World*. New York, NY: Atheneum/Richard Jackson Books.

Mariconda, Barbara. 2014. "Teaching Voice in Writing."http://empoweringwriters.com/teachers-corner/implementation-assistance-faq/tips-and-strategies/teaching-voice-in-writing/.

Markle, Sandra. 1993. Outside and Inside series. New York, NY: Walker and Company.

McAndrew, Donald A., and Thomas J. Reigstad. 2001. *Tutoring Writing: A Practical Guide for Conferences*. Portsmouth, NH: Heinemann.

Merriam-Webster Online Dictionary, s.v. "opinion," Acessed http://www.merriam-webster.com/dictionary/opinion.

Messner, Kate. 2011. *Real Revision: Authors' Strategies to Share with Student Writers*. Portland, ME: Stenhouse Publishers.

Murray, Donald. 1985. *A Writer Teaches Writing*, 2nd ed. Boston, MA: Houghton Mifflin Harcourt.

Myhill, Debra, and Susan Jones. 2007. "More Than Just Error Correction: Students' Perspectives on Their Revision Processes During Writing." *Written Communication* 24 (4): 323–343.

National Council of Teachers of English. 2004. "NCTE Beliefs about the Teaching of Writing." http://www.ncte.org/positions/statements/writingbeliefs.

National Council of Teachers of English. 2013. *You Have a Story to Tell*. http://tinyurl.com/o6tzts6.

National Endowment for the Arts. 2012. "National Endowment for the Arts Presents Highlights from the 2012 Survey of Public Participation in the Arts." http://arts. gov/news/2013/national-endowment-arts-presents-highlights-2012-survey-public-participation-arts#sthash.VsO2oThH.dpuf.

National Governors Association (NGA) Center for Best Practices and Council of Chief State School Officers (CCSSO). 2010a. *Common Core State Standards for English Language Arts and Literacy in History/Social Studies, Science, and Technical Subjects*. Washington, DC: Authors. www.corestandards.org/the-standards.

National Governors Association (NGA) Center for Best Practices and Council of Chief State School Officers (CCSSO). 2010b. "Appendix A." Washington, DC: Authors. www.corestandards.org.

National Governors Association (NGA) Center for Best Practices and Council of Chief State School Officers (CCSSO). 2010c. "Appendix B." Washington, DC: Authors. www.corestandards.org.

National Governors Association (NGA) Center for Best Practices and Council of Chief State School Officers (CCSSO). 2010d. "Appendix C." Washington, DC: Authors. www.corestandards.org.

Newkirk, Thomas. 2012. "How We Really Comprehend Nonfiction." *Educational Leadership* 69 (6): 29–32.

Owlet. 2014. "Using Semicolons and Colons." Accessed October 10. http://owlet.letu. edu/grammarlinks/punctuation/punct2d.html.

Peha, Steve. 2003. *The Five Facts of Fiction: A Fun Way to Write Great Stories and a Great Way to Have Fun Reading Them*. www.ttms.org.

Picard Taylor, Sara. 2008. *A Quick Guide to Teaching Persuasive Writing, K–2*. Portsmouth, NH: Heinemann.

Portalupi, JoAnn, and Ralph Fletcher. 2001. *Nonfiction Craft Lessons: Teaching Information Writing K–8*. Portland, ME: Stenhouse Publishers.

Sanders, Ted J. M., and Joost Schilperoord. 2006. "Text Structure as a Window on the Cognition of Writing: How Text Analysis Provides Insights in Writing Products and Writing Processes." In *Handbook of Writing Research*. Charles A. MacArthur, Steve Graham, and Jill Fitzgerald, eds. 386–402. New York, NY: Guilford Publications, Inc.

Sayre, April Pulley. 2008. *Trout Are Made of Trees*. Watertown, MA: Charlesbridge.

Scardamalia, Marlene, and Carl Bereiter. 1986. "Writing." In *Cognition and Instruction*. Ronna F. Dillon, and Robert J. Sternberg, eds. 59–81 San Diego, CA: Academic Press, Inc.

Shanahan, Timothy. 2012a. "Meeting the Challenge of Common Core: Planning Close Reading." https://sites.google.com/site/tscommoncore/home/close-reading.

Shanahan, Timothy. 2012b. "What Is Close Reading?" http://www.shanahanonliteracy.com/2012/06/what-is-close-reading.html.

Shanahan, Timothy. 2013. "Phases of a Close Reading Lesson." *Reading Today* 39 (6): 15.

Sommers, Nancy. 1980. "Revision Strategies of Student Writers and Experienced Adult Writers." *College Composition and Communication* 31 (4): 378–388.

Spence, Carma. 2011. "Types of Writing: What Is Creative Nonfiction?" http://www.examiner.com/article/types-of-writing-what-is-creative-nonfiction.

Spinner, Jenny. 2004. "When 'Macaroni and Cheese Is Good Enough': Revelation in Creative Nonfiction." *Pedagogy* 4 (2): 316–322.

Waldman, Katy. 2013. "Most American Adults Read Books But Not Literature." *Slate*. http://www.slate.com/blogs/xx_factor/2013/10/01/nea_survey_on_2012_reading_habits_women_continue_to_read_more_than_men.html.

Ward, Helen. 2003. *The Tin Forest*. New York, NY: Dutton Children's Books.

WriteSteps. 2013. "WriteSteps Freebie: Opinion, Persuasive, and Argument Writing Chart." http://writestepswriting.com/eNewsletterArchive/May2013Newsletter.aspx#sthash.PwVZNDnn.dpuf.

Mentor Texts

Bogard, Jenn. 2014. "Giving Back."

Chase, Trevor. 2014. "Dear Mr. and Mrs. Chase."

Coan, Sharon, Jennifer Droll, and Kathleen C. Peterson. 2010. *Read and Succeed: Comprehension*. Huntington Beach, CA: Shell Educational Publishing, Inc.

Ludwig VanDerwater, Amy. 2010. "Sea Glass." http://www.poemfarm.amylv.com/2010/08/mypowriye-148-sea-glass.html.

Ludwig VanDerwater, Amy. 2011. "Asters." http://www.poemfarm.amylv.com/2011/09/asters-writing-about-beauty.html.

Ludwig VanDerwater, Amy. 2011. "Round and Round." http://www.poemfarm.amylv.com/2011/10/round-and-round.html.

Library of Congress. 2014. "The 4th of July in Colorado: A Local Legacy." Accessed October 10. http://www.americaslibrary.gov/es/co/es_co_rodeo_1.html.

Library of Congress. 2014. "Bean-Hole Beans: A Local Legacy." Accessed October 10. http://www.americaslibrary.gov/es/me/es_me_beans_1.html.

Library of Congress. 2014. "The Corn Palace: A Local Legacy." Accessed October 10. http://www.americaslibrary.gov/es/sd/es_sd_corn_1.html.

Library of Congress. 2014. "Louis' Lunch: A Local Legacy." Accessed October 10. http://www.americaslibrary.gov/es/ct/es_ct_burger_1.html.

Library of Congress. 2014. "The Peanut Man." Accessed October 10. http://www.americaslibrary.gov/aa/carver/aa_carver_peanut_1.html.

Markham, Dylyn. 2014. "I Love My Grandpa."

Melino, Alayna. 2014. "Homework Should Be Banned in All Schools."

Piper, Allie. 2014. "Sisters for Life."

Author Interviews

Adler, David - http://www.scholastic.com/teachers/article/david-adler-interview-transcript

Blume, Judy – http://www.cynthialeitichsmith.com/lit_resources/authors/interviews/judyblume.html

Dahl, Roald - http://www.roalddahlmuseum.org/discoverdahl/index.aspx

Fleischman, Paul - http://www.paulfleischman.net/newsletter.htm

Fleischman, Sid - http://www.readingrockets.org/books/interviews/fleischman/
    transcript/

Gantos, Jack - http://www.scholastic.com/teachers/contributor/jack-gantos

Hale, Shannon - http://mass.pbslearningmedia.org/resource/2059d9c3-e1eb-49cf-
    aa7a-5d4bd22ffbca/2059d9c3-e1eb-49cf-aa7a-5d4bd22ffbca/

Konigsburg, E. L. - http://www.scholastic.com/teachers/article/el-konigsburg-
    interview-transcript

Lester, Julius - http://www.scholastic.com/teachers/article/julius-lester-interview-
    transcript

Myers, Walter Dean - http://www.scholastic.com/teachers/article/walter-dean-myers-
    interview-transcript

Naylor, Phyllis - http://www.readingrockets.org/books/interviews/naylor/transcript/

Pearson, Ridley - http://archives.nbclearn.com/portal/site/k-12/
    flatview?cuecard=60886

Rowling, J. K. -http://www.hp-lexicon.org/about/books/books-hp.html

Schachner, Judy - http://www.nbclearn.com/writersspeak

Van Allsburg, Chris - http://www.scholastic.com/teachers/article/chris-van-allsburg-
    interview-transcirpt

Voigt, Cynthia - http://www.scholastic.com/teachers/article/cynthia-voigt-interview-
    transcript.

Woodson, Jacqueline – http://www.nbclearn.com/writersspeak

Yep, Laurence - http://www.scholastic.com/teachers/article/laurence-yep-interview-
    transcirpt

Additional Resources

Classroom Bookshelf – http://classroombookshelf.blogspot.com

NBC Learn: Writers Speak to Kids – http://www.nbclearn.com/writersspeak

Reading Rockets- http://www.readingrockets.org/books/interviews/

Scholastic- http://www.scholastic.com/librarians/ab/biolist.htm

The Poem Farm – http://www.poemfarm.amylv.com

Student Copies—Chapter 2: Narrative Writing
Jottings: "Giving Back"

Name _____ Date _____

Directions: As you read this article, jot down your thoughts.

GIVING BACK

By Jenn Bogard

Edwin zig-zagged through the boundary of beach grass that separated his great-grandfather's old boat shop from the busy freeway. The shop was sheltered by weathered shingles— mostly yellow in color, yet the grays and greens of past generations peeked through. Edwin clasped the handle of the raw, splintered door bitten by years of icy winds and salty sprays. He creaked the door open and peered inside.

The shelves were still lined with gallons of resin and gallons of paint. Resting on the floor was an old cardboard box filled with sketches and secrets of boat building. As Edwin closed his eyes, he remembered thinly sliced curls of wood spiraling to the wide pine floor like pinwheels turning in a summer breeze. "The shop is just the way great-grandpa left it," he thought to himself.

Additional Thoughts:
What do you wonder? What did you discover? What do you want to discuss?

Student Copy
Jottings: "Sisters for Life"

Name _____ Date _____

Directions: As you read this article, jot down your thoughts.

Sisters for Life

By Allie Piper

I curled up in Juliette's lap and hoped time would stop. We sat in silence, staring at the TV. I don't remember what we were watching, but it didn't matter because we weren't watching it anyway. We were just too sad to focus on anything.

My mind drifted back ten months to the very first time I met Juliette, our foreign exchange student who had come all the way from France. I remembered how my heart was beating like a hummingbird's wings as we drove to the hotel to pick her up. I remembered the questions that raced through my mind, "Will she like me?" "Will this be awkward?" "How will we communicate?" "Will we argue like real siblings?" I remembered seeing her chestnut-colored hair, her hazel eyes, and her bright smile with little braces on her teeth. There she was...my new 15-year-old sister, holding a small bag, a big bag, and handbag. I remembered how she gave me a big hug.

My mom interrupted my thoughts, "Kids, it's time for breakfast." But I didn't want it to be time for breakfast.

Sitting at the breakfast table with our five sad faces, it was different than our usual loud, laughing meals. Thinking about all of the travels, silliness, and fun we had together brought a smile to my face. A little giggle slipped out and I said, "I won't ever forget dancing in the elevator in California." Juliette laughed and replied, "or toilet paper volleyball!" Mom and Dad just looked confused because those were *our* secrets. James whined, "Dad, why does Juliette have to leave?"

Soon, the table became silent again. Juliette rested her fork on her plate and began to chew on her fingernails. As I stared at my half-eaten pancake, I imagined myself sitting in the window seat of a plane and hearing the pilot announce, "Welcome to France!" I imagined Juliette guiding me on my own tour of Paris, just like she promised. I imagined eating ham and cheese crepes with her, and I imagined taking the train from Paris to her house.

I leaned over and whispered, "Je t'aime" in Juliette's ear. Juliette hugged me and said, "Sisters for life." In that moment, I knew I would miss her, and I still miss her today.

Additional Thoughts:
What do you wonder? What did you discover? What do you want to discuss?

Student Copy—Chapter 3: Poetry
Jottings: "Round and Round"

Name _____ Date _____

Directions: As you read the poem, jot down your thoughts.

Round and Round

Her beak filled
with twigs
from here
        and there
she gathers
arranges them
into a nest.

Mother Bird lays
three perfect eggs
They hatch.
They grow.
They pass the test
flying away
on fuzzy wings
as Mother Bird
alone
now sings
songs of sun
in southern skies.

The nest blows down.

Mother Bird flies
farfaraway
from her home
on the ground.

Twigs become
nest becomes twigs.

Round and round.
© Amy LV

Additional Thoughts:
What do you wonder? What did you discover? What do you want to discuss?

Student Copy

Jottings: "Sea Glass"

Name _____ Date _____

Directions: As you read the poem, note your thoughts.

Sea Glass

Under
Under
Under the sea
a broken bottle
waits for me.

Water washes
over glass.

Sharp turns
smooth.

Years come.
Years pass.

Someday
somewhere
on a beach
I'll spot a speck
of glass.

I'll reach
down to hold
one frosty stone
polished
by sea
for me
alone.

© Amy LV

Additional Thoughts:
What do you wonder? What did you discover? What do you want to discuss?

Student Copy
Jottings: "Asters"

Name _____ Date _____

Directions: As you read the poem, note your thoughts.

Asters

Summer passed
firefly-fast.
Now dancing asters
have a blast
as golden roadsides
roll in shawls
of fuzzy faces
soft and small.

Violet
fireflake
snowworks
call –

Love now.
We will not last.
It's fall.

© Amy LV

Additional Thoughts:
What do you wonder? What did you discover? What do you want to discuss?

Student Copies—Chapter 4: Informative/ Explanatory Writing

Jottings: "The 4ᵗʰ of July in Colorado"

Name _____ Date _____

Directions: As you read this article, jot down your thoughts.

The 4th of July in Colorado
A Local Legacy (from Library of Congress)

Many American cities have rodeos but Greeley, Colorado, has the "Worlds' Largest Fourth of July Rodeo." The city was named after Horace Greeley, a well-known newspaperman for the New York Tribune. One of his famous sayings was "Go west, Young Man, go west. In 1869, he sent one of his reporters west to Colorado to write a story about farming. The reporter, Nathan C. Meeker, liked the area so much he stayed and started a town named after his boss. It was Meeker's vision that helped establish a successful community based on, among other qualities, cooperation, agriculture, irrigation, and education.

Every year the people of Greeley celebrate Independence Day with a rodeo. In the early days, the rodeo was a small local event, but it grew more and more popular. In 1922, more than 10,000 people came to the rodeo, and the town officially named the event the "Greeley Fourth of July Celebration and the Spud Rodeo and Horseshow." They called it the spud rodeo because spuds (another name for potatoes) are an important crop grown around Greeley. A few years later, even more people came to the rodeo, when famous cowboys started competing with the local ranch hands. Today, the rodeo lasts for two weeks and is called the Greeley Independence Stampede.

Additional Thoughts:
What do you wonder? What did you discover? What do you want to discuss?

Student Copy

Jottings: "The Corn Palace"

Name _____ Date _____

Directions: As you read this article, jot down your thoughts.

The Corn Palace

A Local Legacy
(from Library of Congress)

Imagine a building covered with colorful murals.
Now imagine that same building with an exterior
made entirely out of corn and other grains! This
building exists—it is the Corn Palace.
Built in 1892 in Mitchell, South Dakota, the
Corn Palace was created to dramatically
display the products of the harvest of South
Dakota's farmers, in murals on the outside of
the building. The murals are made from
thousands of bushels of corn and other
grains and grasses such as wild oats, rye,
straw, and wheat. Each year these corn
decorations are completely stripped down
and entirely new murals are created. The
Corn Palace is a great tourist attraction and
a meeting place for the community. Many
events are held here and the most popular is
the Corn Palace Stampede Rodeo. But the
horses must be watched carefully so they
don't eat the building!

Additional Thoughts:
What do you wonder? What did you discover? What do you
want to discuss?

Student Copy
Jottings: "Louis' Lunch"

Name _____ Date _____

Directions: As you read this article, jot down your thoughts.

Louis' Lunch
A Local Legacy
(from Library of Congress)

Do you love hamburgers? Do you know how they were created?

The first hamburgers in U.S. history were served in New Haven, Connecticut, at Louis' Lunch sandwich shop in 1895. Louis Lassen, founder of Louis' Lunch, ran a small lunch wagon selling steak sandwiches to local factory workers. Because he didn't like to waste the excess beef from his daily lunch rush, he ground it up, grilled it, and served it between two slices of bread—and America's first hamburger was created.

The small Crown Street luncheonette is still owned and operated by third and fourth generations of the Lassen family. Hamburgers are still the specialty of the house, where steak is ground fresh each day and hand molded, slow cooked, broiled vertically, and served between two slices of toast with your choice of only three "acceptable" garnishes: cheese, tomato, and onion.

Want ketchup or mustard? Forget it. You will be told "no" in no uncertain terms. This is the home of the greatest hamburger in the world, claim the owners, who are perhaps best known for allowing their customers to have a burger the "Lassen way" or not at all.

Additional Thoughts:
What do you wonder? What did you discover? What do you want to discuss?

#51482—Writing is Magic, Or Is It?

Student Copy
Jottings: "Bean-Hole Beans"

Name _____ Date _____

Directions: As you read this article, jot down your thoughts.

Bean-Hole Beans
A Local Legacy
(from Library of Congress)

What's a bean-hole bean? No, it's not a bean with a hole in it. Bean-hole beans get their name because they are baked in a hole. For hundreds of years, the Penobscot Indians of Maine cooked their food in a hole in the ground. The first thing you need to cook bean-hole beans is a shovel!

Recipe for bean-hole beans:

-Dig a hole in the ground 3 feet deep and line it with rocks.

-Build a fire in the hole and let it burn down to large embers and ash. (This can take half a day before enough coals are produced to cook the beans properly.)

-Use dry beans such as Great Northern, Yellow Eye, Jacob's Cattle, or Soldier.

-Other ingredients include onions, salt pork, ham hock, bacon, tomatoes, brown sugar and molasses.

Put the beans and other ingredients in a cast iron pot and cover with water and a lid. Place the pot in the hole, cover with a wet dish towel or burlap sack, shovel some of the embers and ashes on top of the pot, and then cover with dirt. Cooking time varies depending on which recipe is used but, it can take as long as 16 hours. Then get ready with a shovel and a bowl!

Additional Thoughts:
What do you wonder? What did you discover? What do you want to discuss?

Student Copies—Chapter 5: Narrative Nonfiction
Jottings: "The Peanut Man"

Name _____ Date _____

Directions: As you read this article, jot down your thoughts.

The Peanut Man
A Local Legacy
(from Library of Congress)

George Washington Carver was always interested in plants. When he was a child, he was known as the "plant doctor." He had a secret garden where he grew all kinds of plants. People would ask him for advice when they had sick plants. Sometimes he'd take their plants to his garden and nurse them back to health. (paragraph 1)

Later, when he was teaching at Tuskegee Institute, he put his plant skills to good use. Many people in the South had been growing only cotton on their land. Cotton plants use most of the nutrients in the soil. (Nutrients provide nourishment to plants.) So the soil becomes "worn out" after a few years. Eventually, cotton will no longer grow on this land. (paragraph 2)

This was especially bad for poor African American farmers, who relied on selling cotton to support themselves. Carver was dedicated to helping those farmers, so he came up with a plan. (paragraph 3)

Carver knew that certain plants put nutrients back into the soil. One of those plants is the peanut! Peanuts are also a source of protein. (paragraph 4)

Carver thought that if those farmers planted peanuts, the plants would help restore their soil, provide food for their animals, and provide protein for their families—quite a plant! In 1896 peanuts were not even recognized as a crop in the United States, but Carver would help change that. (paragraph 5)

#51482—Writing is Magic, Or Is It?

Carver told farmers to rotate their crops: plant cotton one year, then the next year plant peanuts and other soil-restoring plants, like peas and sweet potatoes. It worked! The peanut plants grew and produced lots of peanuts. The plants added enough nutrients to the soil so cotton grew the next year. Now the farmers had lots of peanuts—too many for their families and animals—and no place to sell the extras. Again, Carver had a plan. Do you know what he did? (paragraph 6)

Carver invented all kinds of things made out of peanuts. He wrote down more than 300 uses for peanuts, including peanut milk, peanut paper, and peanut soap. Carver thought that if farmers started making things out of peanuts, they'd have to buy fewer things and would be more self-sufficient. And if other people started making things out of peanuts, they would want to buy the extra peanuts, so the farmers would make more money. Although not many of Carver's peanut products were ever mass-produced, he did help spread the word about peanuts. (paragraph 7)

Peanuts became more and more popular. By 1920 there were enough peanut farmers to form the United Peanut Association of America (UPAA). In 1921 the UPAA asked Carver to speak to the U.S. Congress about the many uses for peanuts. Soon the whole country had heard of George Washington Carver, the Peanut Man! And by 1940 peanuts had become one of the top six crops in the U.S. (paragraph 8)

Additional Thoughts:
What do you wonder? What did you discover? What do you want to discuss?

Mentor Text: "Confucius, the Great Chinese" Philosopher

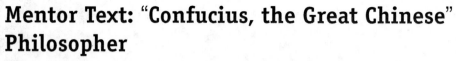

Confucius, the Great Chinese Philosopher

Confucius, the Great Chinese Philosopher
Coan, Sharon, Jennifer Droll, and Kathleen C. Peterson.

In China long ago lived a man named Confucius. His teachings changed Chinese culture, and his influence continues today. Great thinkers called philosophers wondered about their laws and questioned, "Is this really right?" Confucius was one of these thinkers.

Confucius read many books that helped him think of ways in which his government could improve. He saw how the poor starved when the harvests failed. He watched the government abuse its power. Confucius wanted to help those in need, and he wanted to end wars. He devoted his life to this cause.

Confucius started a school and invited both nobles and peasants to learn. This was shocking. At that time, people believed that only nobles could be educated. Confucius knew that education could make people equal. His school was free. It had just one requirement: each student had to love learning.

Confucius taught his students that the government should help everyone have good lives. Rulers should earn their power through their concern for their people. He told his students to speak out against dishonest, corrupt rulers. It's not surprising that some rulers disliked him.

China would not be what it is today without Confucius's teachings. Other societies have followed his ideas as well. If Confucius were alive today, he would be amazed. He died thinking that he had not changed China. Yet he had changed the world.

Additional Thoughts:
What do you wonder? What did you discover? What do you want to discuss?

Student Copies—Chapter 6: Opinion/Argument Writing

Jottings: "I Love my Grandpa" (Opinion)

Name _____ Date _____

Directions: As you read this article, jot down your thoughts.

I Love my Grandpa

By Dylyn Markham

"Bye, Dylyn, have a great day," said my grandpa to me. When I hear him say that every morning, I think to myself, "My life is great with my grandpa."

He is patient. A lot of the time my brother stomps on the table. Instead of screaming my grandpa asks, "Will you please get off the table"?

Most of the time my grandpa goes into stores with long lines. Instead of cutting people to get to the front, he waits patiently for his turn. Sometimes my grandpa has some trouble with his car. Instead of blaming it on someone else, he calmly fixes it. Also, he is a hard worker. Sometimes my grandpa mows the lawn and that is hard work because in the summer it is so hot. My grandpa fixes stuff when it needs fixing. A lot of times he fixed our computer, my Go Cart or some electronics.

My grandpa helps me with anything like my pitching, my wrestling moves, or my homework. Truly he has a great sense of humor. Yesterday my brother and my grandpa were playing bowling on the Wii when my grandpa said, "I am going to win," and my brother said, "In your dreams" and my grandpa started cracking up laughing. My grandpa is always telling jokes at dinner. My grandpa has a great laugh. When my grandpa laughs, I know it is him. Grandpas make life better.

Additional Thoughts:
What do you wonder? What did you discover? What do you want to discuss?

Student Copy
Jottings: "Dear Mr. and Mrs. Chase" (Persuasion)

Name _____ Date _____

Directions: As you read this article, jot down your thoughts.

Dear Mr. and Mrs. Chase,

Have you been feeling Trevor is bored with his daily life? Have you found yourself wanting to shake things up a bit at home? I, myself, think that your son, Trevor Chase, should be able to get a lizard. Yes, lizards are unique pets but they are easily contained and could help teach Trevor some more responsibility, not that he already isn't responsible.

The lizard will teach Trevor responsibility by letting him clean its cage and holding it with care. Trevor will become a smarter kid with the learning the lizard will give him. The lizard will be medium level care, so he won't have to take care of the lizard 24/7 and he will still have time to play all the sports he does. Trevor will still need to do the basic care though. If he could play with a lizard, he wouldn't be bugging you all the time. If Trevor could get a lizard, he would be playing less video games and spending more time with his lizard and his friends. This would be a great choice for everyone. This might be a bad idea because he may want to experiment with his lizard. I understand that your family has a dog, so just make sure none of Trevor's friends try to feed the dog.

Maybe Trevor is having a hard time focusing on homework because all that is going through his mind is that lizard. Maybe he will be able to focus knowing there is a lizard named Stevie waiting in his room. There is also a downside to that. He would always be wanting to see his lizard. He will learn that Stevie will not be going anywhere and the lizard will still be there when Trevor goes to see him. Trevor can also have an educational experience from learning about lizards. Trevor could do many reports on lizards and even give the audience a little treat about the report.

I believe that lizards are easy to maintain. They need care and the right temperature to survive. Lizards are pretty tough animals so they do not need your care all of the time. I think Trevor will be able to feed Stevie once a day, and he also will have to work hard for money for a nice cage and lamp so his cage will be just like in the wild. Trevor will need to clean the cage about every week or so to keep Stevie and Trevor happy. The downside to this is that since Trevor plays many sports, he might not have the time to clean the cage every week but I believe that he will be just fine.

Trevor is a good kid as I have heard, but maybe a lizard will make him even better. Even though it may be a little extra work, I personally think it is worth it. I personally have a Komodo Dragon, which is one of the biggest lizards on the planet. Even a lizard that big isn't that hard to take care of. The last thing I have to say is that Trevor will be happy with his new friend, Stevie. I hope this will convince you!

Thank you for reading.

Yours truly,

Trevor

Additional Thoughts:
What do you wonder? What did you discover? What do you want to discuss?

Student Copy

Jottings: "Homework Should be Banned in all Schools" (Argument)

Name _____ Date _____

Directions: As you read this article, jot down your thoughts.

Homework Should be Banned in all Schools

By Alayna Melino

A 2004 study by the University of Michigan says that homework time is up 51% since 1981. Some 13 year olds are spending over 2 hours a night on homework. Students in grades 3-6 spend around 30-60 minutes a night. High schoolers spend on average 30 minutes per class, which sometimes adds up to 3.5 hours (DeNisco). According to the guidelines by the National Education Association, a student shouldn't spend more than 10 minutes per grade level per night. That means that 7th graders should only be spending 70 minutes but that's often doubled or even tripled (Morin). In Finland students receive no homework and their high school graduate rate is 93% compared to the US, which is 75% (Biljalk). Homework should be banned in all schools.

Students who receive lots of homework are the ones who usually get the most stressed out. Many kids break down emotionally, physically, and mentally under stress and most of it is coming from their schoolwork. They cry, get sick, and sometimes even puke on their test books. A 2007 American Academy of Pediatrics report claims that too much work for children and too little play could backfire down the road (Kam). Also, colleges are seeing lots of students who are showing signs of depression, perfectionism, and stress. Lee Bartel, a professor at the University of Toronto, did a study on the effects of homework and how it causes anxiety and stress. He took data from over 20,000 kids and the results showed that homework causes much stress and leads to many breakdowns and therefore it is just useless (Kam). It is only doing harm to the students and is even causing parents to stress out too. Homework is stress and anxiety that students do not need.

Additional Thoughts:
What do you wonder? What did you discover? What do you want to discuss?

#51482—Writing is Magic, Or Is It?

Writing Strategies

Chapter 2: Narrative Writing

Snapshot: When we use a camera, we take a snapshot to allow others to see exactly what we see. Writers can do this with words. A snapshot is a detailed physical description of what you want your readers to see in his or her mind (Lane 1993). For example, authors might write a snapshot to show the physical details of a character's expression, the physical details of a place, or the physical details of a building.

Simile: A simile is a figure of speech. The writer compares two things by using the word like or by using the word as. The purpose of a simile is to paint a clear picture in the reader's mind by drawing on something the reader likely knows. You might have heard the similes: as cute as a button or eats like a bird.

Thoughtshot: In order to create a thoughtshot, writers stop the action for a brief moment and reveal what a character is thinking or feeling (Lane 1993). Thoughtshots allow the reader to hear the exact words that the character is thinking. Writers often signal the use of a thoughtshot with phrases including, I thought to myself or I kept thinking or I said to myself or I wondered. The exact thoughts are written in quotations or in italics.

Flashback: Although some stories are written entirely in the form of a flashback, students can also insert a flashback that is a relatively quick moment in the writing piece—a paragraph or so—in which the character remembers something meaningful that happened in the past. According to Fletcher & Portalupi (2007), "glimpses into the past can be used to develop character, invite readers into significant moments gone by, or make contrasts that point to important changes that have occurred (113).

Transitional Phrases to Signal a Flashback: Flashbacks are often signaled with phrases that ease transition for readers such as, I remember one time when or I remembered back to the time when or Once when I was or My mind traveled back to when.

Flash-Forward: In order to provide readers with a glimpse into the future, writers can stop the chronological sequence of the events in a piece of writing and transition to a flash-forward. In a flash-forward, the character or narrator imagines a key event that could happen but has not yet happened. A flash-forward can be as short as a couple of sentences. These meaningful scenes are often signaled by phrases that that ease transition for readers such as, I imagined myself... or I began to think about... or My mind drifted to the future....

AAAWWUBBIS Words: (After, Although, As, When, While, Until, Because, Before, If, Since)

AAAWWUBBIS serves as a mnemonic device for recalling subordinating conjunctions. A subordinating conjunction allows the dependent clause to join the main clause in order to express meaning. When a sentence begins with an AAAWWUBBIS word, writers usually need to use a comma after the opening phrase (unless the main clause is very short). Writers can use AAAWWUBBIS words to create sentence variety.

In addition to the word although, the words even though and though also count as AAAWWUBBIS words, and in addition to the word when, the word whenever counts (Anderson 2005).

Dialogue and Dialogue Tags: Dialogue can be used to move the story along and to control the pacing, to reveal character's motivations, and to reveal a relationship among characters. Dialogue tags are also used to express a character's feelings or intent. For example, the dialogue tag, "with tears in her eyes" shows that the character does not want to leave her dog in the following sentence: "I hope to see you soon, Frank," whispered Lucy with tears in her eyes.

Emotional Ending: The ending of a story is the last thing readers are left with. When a writer decides to write a story that shows strong emotion, it can be powerful to match the ending to the emotion conveyed throughout the story (Fletcher and Portalupi 2007).

Chapter 3: Poetry

Word Choice: By choosing precise words with purpose, writers clarify meaning and provide details. Precise word choice allows readers to create mental images in their mind and can be used to show a character's motivations or feelings.

Line Breaks: Students are often surprised to find how they can emphasize, or even change, meaning by playing with the lines breaks of a poem. The decision of where to end a line within a poem impacts the message they want to convey.

Alliteration: The repetition of beginning consonant sounds can be used to convey the mood of what is happening in a poem. Alliteration also creates pacing—how quickly or slowly the reader reads a section of the poem.

Circular Ending: A circular ending is when the writer begins and ends his or her writing piece by repeating a meaningful word, phrase, or idea. Circular endings can be used to highlight a character's realization or to mirror a cycle of change within the content of the poem.

Varying Length of Stanzas: Poets might follow a long stanza with short stanza or vice versa to create mood or to emphasize a point. By juxtaposing long and short stanzas, the writer can contrast moments in a poem or highlight a change in events or a change within a character.

Repetition: By repeating specific words or phrases, a writer can convey rhythm and movement and show the passage of time.

Syllables: Syllables can be used to establish the mood of the events of characters in a poem.

Strong Verbs: Strong verbs allow the reader to picture the specific actions of characters, objects, or forces in a poem. Strong verbs also convey exact expressions, feelings, or motivations of the characters.

Varying the Length of Sentences: Short sentences might communicate ideas such as time passing quickly. Short sentences can also be used to emphasize a message. By juxtaposing short and long sentences, writers can address feelings, events, and pacing.

Personification: By giving human qualities to nonliving things or to inanimate objects or forces, writers can paint a picture in the reader's mind, showing their behavior, attitude, actions, intentions and more.

Metaphor: A metaphor is a figure of speech in which the author uses one thing to represent another. The reader infers the implied relationship. The use of metaphor activates the senses and imagination, highlighting meaning for the reader. You might have heard of the metaphors *icing on the cake* or *breath of fresh air*.

Point of View (first person): By speaking directly to the reader, the writer can communicate important life messages and encourage readers to connect to the text.

Chapter 4: Informative/Explanatory Writing

"I Think": Students use this lead strategy to create a comprehensive opening sentence that reveals the topic of the text and what the author thinks about this topic.

Show, Don't Tell: As the name suggests, this strategy allows writers to show rather than explicitly state the information they share.

Commas with Non-essential Information: This strategy explores how and why writers weave in phrases that contain interesting, but not critical, information.

Commanding Leads: This common lead strategy hooks readers by drawing them directly into the text. Words such as "Imagine" or "Look at" are often used.

Begin with a Verb: As a way to add variety to sentence beginnings, this strategy invites students to play with verbs as sentence openers.

Building Bridges Between Ideas: This transition strategy enables writers to create cohesion between and among sentences by paying attention to how the sentences work together.

Why/How?: This common nonfiction organizational strategy focuses on why a new idea or invention was useful or necessary, and how it was realized.

Adding Details with Adverbs: This strategy focuses on using adverbs to tell why, how, when, and under what condition something is happening or has happened.

Why a Colon?: Colons often signal a list, which is the grammar generalization introduced in this strategy.

Concluding with a Claim: A claim is what someone believes to be true. "Conclude with a Claim" enables writers to bring closure to an informative text by stating one (indisputable) truth about the topic.

Imperatives: This strategy offers writers opportunities to add specificity to their texts by calling attention to imperatives (command words) used in procedural writing (e.g., *stir, rake, gather*).

"How-to" Organization: "How-to" texts generally follow a recognizable organizational formula, which is introduced through this strategy.

Ta-da!: Often, the conclusion of a procedural piece of writing contains a statement that applauds the reader for successfully completing the directions. The "Ta-da!" strategy encourages writers to show excitement and conclude with a bit of fanfare.

Chapter 5: Narrative Nonfiction

Factual Information vs the Author's Personal Response/Reaction/Reflections: This strategy helps writers differentiate between facts (truths) and opinions that authors of literary nonfiction typically integrate into their texts.

Voice, Tone, and Mood: With this strategy, we explore how writers of narrative nonfiction achieve a voice, tone, and mood that is characteristic of this genre.

Coordinating Conjunctions (FANBOYS): For, And, Nor, But, Or, Yet, and So are coordinating conjunctions that link two independent clauses (i.e., complete sentences). Commas are generally used with each conjunction to separate the clauses.

White Space: Writers must decide whether to indent paragraphs or leave white spaces between paragraphs. Either style is acceptable, but writers should not alternate between the two. In this strategy, we explore the purposes of creating paragraphs in written texts.

Fulfilling a Promise: This strategy (created by Muriel Harris as cited in McAndrew and Reigstad 2001, 44), points to the fact that authors make a promise to readers to write about one topic or thesis. Students determine what promise an author makes and evaluate how parts of the text help fulfill the promise.

Word Choice - Strong Verbs: In this strategy, we explore strong verbs and why they are important in narrative nonfiction writing.

Chapter 6: Opinion/Argument Writing

Concluding Statement: For One and All: When writers end with a concise statement that reiterates the main point of the writing piece, readers are left with a clear take-away message.

Highlight to Group Reasons and their Examples: Color can help writers group and organize related ideas in order to present a logically sequenced writing piece, providing clarity and minimizing confusion.

Words and Phrases that Speak to the Heart: When writing an opinion piece about an emotional topic, writers can use words and phrases that are full of emotion and tug at the reader's heart. This way, the reader understands the writer's opinion.

Speak Directly to Your Audience: Some believe that all opinion/argument writing should have an objective tone, but this is not the case. Speaking directly to your target audience and communicating your personality can help to create a powerfully convincing piece.

Questioning Lead: Writers can spark interest and activate their readers' ideas about the topic of discussion by asking relevant questions at the start of the writing piece.

Recognize Different Perspectives: Acknowledging and addressing viewpoints that differ from those presented can actually help to strengthen the overall claims of the piece. These alternate viewpoints can become counter arguments in which the writer discusses and refutes opposing views.

Use a Thesis Statement: Stating the claim of the argument in one concise and clear sentence helps to orient readers as they read the examples, opinions, and other support throughout the piece. Thesis statements should come in the beginning of the writing piece.

Consult a Credible Source: Facts, statistics, and information from interviews can help to provide objective support for a claim. Sources should be credible and cited within the text.

Stay Focused: It is important for writers of opinion and argument essays to stay focused on one topic throughout each text. Doing so allows the writer to develop one controlling idea and enables the reader to comprehend the writer's message.

***Who* versus *That*:** Grammar Convention: *Who* is used when writers talk about people. *That* is used when referring to an object.

Complete Texts of Excerpts

Giving Back (Chapter 3)

Sisters for Life (Chapter 3)

Homework Should be Banned in all Schools (Chapter 6)

GIVING BACK

by Jenn Bogard

Edwin zig-zagged through the boundary of beach grass that separated his great-grandfather's old boat shop from the busy freeway. The shop was sheltered by weathered shingles—mostly yellow in color, yet the grays and greens of past generations peeked through. Edwin clasped the handle of the raw, splintered door bitten by years of icy winds and salty sprays. He creaked the door open and peered inside.

The shelves were still lined with gallons of resin and gallons of paint. Resting on the floor was an old cardboard box filled with sketches and secrets of boat building. As Edwin closed his eyes, he remembered thinly sliced curls of wood spiraling to the wide pine floor like pinwheels turning in a summer breeze. "The shop is just the way great-grandpa left it," he thought to himself.

The high and low pitches of a cheerful melody chimed four times from the wooden clock on the wall. Edwin noticed a pile of wood scraps scattered by the woodstove and examined the pieces of wood one by one, setting each one to the side.

Finally, he found a piece that had been stained a familiar russet tone. "This will make a great hull," he thought. He brushed off the cobwebs and rested it on the workbench. He began to look for more supplies. "I need a white sail," he thought, "Great-grandpa's sails were white." Edwin saw a fold of canvas under the dusty wooden sawhorse in the corner of the shop. He pulled it out, opened it up, gave it a good shake, and saw right away that it was freckled with tiny holes. "This will work," he thought.

The afternoon light had dimmed and the seagulls' caw seemed far off. Edwin set the canvas beside the wood and added a roll of string to the pile. "I'll be back again after school tomorrow," Edwin said to himself. "My model is going to look just like great-grandpa's boat!"

The next afternoon, Edwin pulled open the old splintered door again.

Crrr-eak

On his way toward the workbench, he paused to admire the newspaper article that was tacked to the corkboard. It was a picture of great-grandpa standing knee-deep in the brackish water, beside a boat that was ready for launching.

Edwin hurried to the workbench with excitement but stopped short. "Where is my hull?" he said. "Where is my canvas? And the string is missing too." Edwin peered under the workbench then glanced around the shop. "That's strange," thought Edwin.

The clock chimed four times. Edwin pulled a sheet of paper from his pocket and read the words: *wood glue, scissors, sandpaper.* "I'll look in the cabinet up in the loft for these supplies," he thought. As Edwin neared closer and closer to the stairs, he felt a quick bolt of fear from the height of the open loft. He remembered the words of his great-grandfather: "Watch your step. The stairs are steep."

Edwin stepped onto the first stair and looked up. There, on the step above, was a tiny white speck of the missing canvas. "That's funny," whispered Edwin. Stepping onto the second floor, Edwin was startled by a loud creak of the floorboard. He looked down and saw a cardboard tube with tiny chew marks tucked right below the floorboard. "That looks like the tube from my string!" said Edwin, scratching his head.

"Is anyone up here?" called Edwin. "Anyone here?" he called again. Edwin heard some rustling. He squinted, but the darkness was too deep. He heard a faint chirping.

Edwin tugged on the hanging string and a bare light bulb lit up the loft. There in the corner, a bird and her babies were nesting. String was threaded throughout the twigs. "You needed the string," whispered Edwin.

He lifted up the floorboard again and reached down for the cardboard tube. Shreds of canvas cushioned the space. The tube felt heavier than he remembered. He peered inside and saw two tiny eyes and pink wrinkly skin.

"A baby mouse!" Edwin cried. "The mice needed the tube," he said to himself. He set the baby mouse back into the snuggly nest beneath the floor.

Edwin smiled and started down the steep stairs with a new idea. He returned to the pile of wood scraps to search for four large boards. Just as he was about to toss the unwanted pieces to the side, he stopped and said out loud, "Does anyone live in here?" A spider scurried deeper into the scraps.

Edwin hurried back to the workbench. He wrote on his list, *Project Two: build homes for the mice, birds, and spiders.* "Tomorrow is Saturday," Edwin thought, "I'll get here by eight, just like great-grandpa used to."

Sisters for Life

By Allie Piper

When I opened my eyes on the morning I had to say goodbye, I felt miserable, and I had an awful feeling in the pit of my stomach. Juliette was leaving. I moped down the stairs like Eeyore to find my dad making pancakes and sausage – our last meal together as a family of five. As my Mom was setting the table, she turned to look at me. With a quiet and sad voice, she said, "Good Morning, Allie." My younger brother, James, was sitting beside Juliette on the couch. They were both sulking. I guess we were all feeling gloomy.

I curled up in Juliette's lap and hoped time would stop. We sat in silence, staring at the TV. I don't remember what we were watching, but it didn't matter because we weren't watching it anyway. We were just too sad to focus on anything.

My mind drifted back ten months to the very first time I met Juliette, our foreign exchange student who had come all the way from France. I remembered how my heart was beating like a hummingbird's wings as we drove to the hotel to pick her up. I remembered the questions that raced through my mind, "Will she like me?" "Will this be awkward?" "How will we communicate?" "Will we argue like real siblings?" I remembered seeing her chestnut-colored hair, her hazel eyes, and her bright smile with little braces on her teeth. There she was...my new 15-year-old sister, holding a small bag, a big bag, and handbag. I remembered how she gave me a big hug.

My mom interrupted my thoughts, "Kids, it's time for breakfast." But I didn't want it to be time for breakfast.

Sitting at the breakfast table with our five sad faces, it was different than our usual loud, laughing meals. Thinking about all of the travels, silliness, and fun we had together brought a smile to my face. A little giggle slipped out and I said, "I won't ever forget dancing in the elevator in California." Juliette laughed and replied, "or toilet paper volleyball!" Mom and Dad just looked confused because those were *our* secrets. James whined, "Dad, why does Juliette have to leave?"

Soon, the table became silent again. Juliette rested her fork on her plate and began to chew on her fingernails. As I stared at my half-eaten pancake, I imagined myself sitting in the window seat of a plane and hearing the pilot announce, "Welcome to France!" I imagined Juliette guiding me on my own tour of Paris, just like she promised. I imagined eating ham and cheese crepes with her, and I imagined taking the train from Paris to her house.

I leaned over and whispered, "Je t'aime" in Juliette's ear. Juliette hugged me and said, "Sisters for life." In that moment, I knew I would miss her, and I still miss her today.

Homework Should be Banned in all Schools

By Alayna Melino

A 2004 study by the University of Michigan says that homework time is up 51% since 1981. Some 13 year olds are spending over 2 hours a night on homework. Students in grades 3-6 spend around 30-60 minutes a night. High schoolers spend on average 30 minutes per class, which sometimes adds up to 3.5 hours (DeNisco). According to the guidelines by the National Education Association, a student shouldn't spend more than 10 minutes per grade level per night. That means that 7th graders should only be spending 70 minutes but that's often doubled or even tripled (Morin). In Finland students receive no homework and their high school graduate rate is 93% compared to the US, which is 75% (Biljalk). Homework should be banned in all schools.

Students who receive lots of homework are the ones who usually get the most stressed out. Many kids break down emotionally, physically, and mentally under stress and most of it is coming from their schoolwork. They cry, get sick, and sometimes even puke on their test books. A 2007 American Academy of Pediatrics report claims that too much work for children and too little play could backfire down the road (Kam). Also, colleges are seeing lots of students who are showing signs of depression, perfectionism, and stress. Lee Bartel, a professor at the University of Toronto, did a study on the effects of homework and how it causes anxiety and stress. He took data from over 20,000 kids and the results showed that homework causes much stress and leads to many breakdowns and therefore it is just useless (Kam). It is only doing harm to the students and is even causing parents to stress out too. Homework is stress and anxiety that students do not need.

Homework is taking up time for activities and family time. Some kids don't even have time to come to dinner due to homework. About 65% of kids 6-13 play competitive sports (Falk). Some of them are quitting the sport they love because they clearly have no time with all their homework. Children need to spend time outside, play sports, spend time with family, etc. But when are they supposed to have time to be a kid when they get hours of homework? Relaxation and down time are very important to children's health. They need time to just lie down and not have the pressure of homework on their shoulders. Most colleges look for students who have the most extra curricular activities and those who participate in sports but with all this homework most kids won't be able to take part in them. A study by the American College of Sports Medicine discovered that less fit students received grades that were 13-20% lower than their classmates (Falk). Kids need to have the time to be active or else their grades and health could drop. Family time and activities need to be the first priority and homework is stopping that.

Students who stay up late doing homework don't get much sleep. Even though homework may help kids who need extra help, a good night sleep is more important.

Teens are on average supposed to get around 8.5-9 hours of sleep each night but that isn't possible if they are up to 11 or 12 pm studying. Only about 8 % of high school students get the sleep that they need. The National Youth Risk Behavior Survey found that 10% of students sleep only 5 hours and 23% only sleep 6 hours a night on an average school night (Carpenter). Studying late at night tired is proven to just weaken your test grade. A student who stays up all night to finish an essay is proven to grasp less of what's being taught the next day in math. What is the point of giving homework if it's just going to weaken test scores by sleep deprivation? Lack of sleep can also cause many health problems like depression, obesity, risk of heart attack and weakens the immune system. Some students even get up early in the morning to finish their work. About 28% of all teenagers say they are too tired to do any physical activity and another 28% of them fall asleep at least once a week in class (Carpenter). Homework is affecting the sleep of many teenagers.

Homework has many negative affects on students. It is causing a lot of unnecessary stress and anxiety. Homework is stopping kids from participating in sports and other school activities. Lack of sleep from staying up late studying is affecting teens' health and sleep patterns. Students who have lots of homework have either worse or the same test scores as students who receive no homework. This proves that homework is just a waste of time and it is doing more harm than it is good. Kids need time to be kids and do the activities they want without having to stress about homework. Homework should be banned in all schools.

References from the Mentor Texts

(for "Homework Should Be Banned in All Schools")

District Administration. Alison DeNisco, Mar. 2013. Web 4 Dec. 2013. http://www.districtadministration.com/article/homework-or-not-research-question

Fox Point- BaysidePatch. Lance J. Falk, Apr. 2012. Web. 4 Dec. 2013. http://foxpoint.patch.com/groups/opinion/p/opinion-too-much-homework-leaves-no-time-to-be-a-kid

Health and Parenting. Katherine Kam, n.d. Web. 4 Dec 2013. http://www.webmd.com/parenting/features/coping-school-stress

NeoMam Studios. Marina Biljak, 4 Mar. 2013 Web. 4 Dec. 2013. http://neomam.com/infographics/there-is-no-homework-in-finland

Should homework be banned? N.p., 2013. Web. 18 Nov. 2013. http://www.debate.org/opinions/should-homework-be-banned

American Pychological Association. Siri Carpenter, n.d. Web. 4 Dec. 2013 http://www.apa.org/monitor/oct01/sleepteen.aspx

Contents of the Digital Resource CD

Page(s)	Resource	Filename
161	Jottings: "Giving Back"	giving.pdf giving.docx
162	Jottings: "Sister For Life"	sisters.pdf sisters.docx
163	Jottings: "Round and Round"	round.pdf round.docx
164	Jottings: "Sea Glass"	seaglass.pdf seaglass.docx
165	Jottings: "Asters"	asters.pdf asters.docx
166	Jottings: "The 4th of July in Colorado"	july.pdf july.docx
167	Jottings: "The Corn Palace"	cornpalace.pdf cornpalace.docx
168	Jottings: "Louis' Lunch"	louis.pdf louis.docx
169	Jottings: "Bean-Hole Beans"	beans.pdf beans.docx
170–171	Jottings: "The Peanut Man"	peanut.pdf peanut.docx
172	Jottings: "Confucius, the Great Chinese Philosopher"	philosopher.pdf philosopher.docx
173	Jottings: "I Love my Grandpa"	grandpa.pdf grandpa.docx
174–175	Jottings: "Dear Mr. and Mrs. Chase"	chase.pdf chase.docx
176	Jottings: "Homework Should be Banned in all Schools"	homework.pdf homework.docx
182–183	"Giving Back"	givingfull.pdf
184	"Sisters for Lite"	sistersfull.pdf
185–186	"Homework Should be Banned in all Schools	homeworkfull.pdf

Notes

Notes

Notes

Notes